The Turning Point *for* Humanity

A Guide to Healing Yourself and Transforming Our World

Elizabeth Grace

Seshat Press
211 Pauline Drive #513
York, PA 17402
www.seshatpress.com
Send questions to: support@seshatpress.com

Paperback ISBN: 979-8-9996544-5-8
Ebook ISBN: 979-8-9996544-6-5
Library of Congress Control Number: 2026902578

Cover artwork inspired by Rebecca Harwin

Printed in the United States of America

Seshat Press is proud to be a part of the Tree Neutral® program. Tree Neutral offsets the number of trees consumed in the production and printing of this book by taking proactive steps such as planting trees in direct proportion to the number of trees used to print books. To learn more about Tree Neutral, please visit treeneutral.com.

*To our beautiful family of humanity
to know itself as the noble race it was designed to be,
to rise above these times of extreme challenge, and
to triumph to create the beautiful kind world we sense is possible,
where all life is honoured as sacred and
we flourish as individuals and collectively.*

CONTENTS

INTRODUCTION

Why Now?

Welcome Dear Reader,

I am so grateful this book has found its way to you and that you are considering exploring different possibilities for your life. We are living through extremely challenging times, and everything is in flux. The world as we have known it is breaking apart at the seams. It has been a dysfunctional, unjust, and unsustainable system for too long and seems to be imploding. There is a great need for new and fairer life-supporting systems to be created. The new beautiful Earth being created in our Hearts and imaginations is not quite visible yet, so everything is uncertain and unpredictable.

We are in paradigm-shifting times, and you may be feeling some big emotions, such as fear, anger, and confusion. You may have big questions around what you are witnessing in the world. It's understandable; these are intense times, and everything is being called into question. To build the resilience required to navigate your way through an ever-changing landscape over the next few years, it is essential to get to know yourself more deeply and to learn new tools and practices to bring your body, mind, and emotions into balance in order to set your spirit free. You cannot control much of the outer world, but you can influence your experience of it by taking charge of your inner environment. The only way out is to go within.

The Impulse of Life

The impulse of life is tapping us all on the shoulder to evolve, to change our way of living and our thinking, and to get back into right relationship with ourselves, nature, and a higher intelligence. There is much potential in you that is calling to be unleashed to reveal the Heart-centred powers of connection, courage, and creativity within you, to heal the hurts and pain and transform them into purpose, and to create the deeper meaning in your life that you yearn for. Now is the time to take charge of your own life, to do what it takes to balance and heal yourself, and to reconnect with your beautiful Heart, your true guidance system.

This is the inner work that needs to be done to effect the changes in the external world we all want to see.

When you heal your wounds, restore your vitality and sanity, and uncover and acknowledge your innate, unique genius qualities, you give permission for others to do the same. There is no greater gift than to know yourself, because then you cannot be coerced, bullied, shamed, or led astray from the path you were meant to live because you now stand as your True Self.

I hope this book will assist you in moving forward in whatever way is best for you so that you may help midwife into existence the beautiful new world we can imagine is possible.

What if the truth is that you were born for this time?

What if this is the time for the different thinkers who lead from the Heart, bringing soul-centred solutions forward?

What if no one else is coming to save us? What if it is up to us?

What if you could be an answered prayer for many others?

What if you chose to be here at the greatest opportunity for change, renewal, revelation, and re-creation to create a new world for the majesty of humanity to rise and flourish again?

The Power of Your Light

The power of your Light, that divine part of your consciousness, is extraordinary and will strengthen and guide you. You are a powerful creator.

What we think, believe, feel, do, and say influences how we experience the world. Many of us are or have been unconscious co-creators and have contributed to the way our world has been operating through our unconscious complacency when times are good and compliance when times are tough.

We do not know ourselves and the power that we are; therefore, we think we are powerless. Then we are easier to control, to be herded in particular directions that do not serve our health or happiness. Together—through our unconscious agreement and deliberately orchestrated ignorance—we have allowed governments, corporations, and institutions to take charge of almost every facet of our lives. But the veil is lifting. Illusions are dissolving, and people are beginning to see through the deception of our leaders. Our world is ripe for change. It has already begun.

Will you be a conscious part of that change?

Through becoming more conscious of our choices and how they serve us—or don't—we can make different decisions that lead to very different outcomes. When we change our thinking, we change our habits. When we change our habits, we change our lives. When we change our lives, we change our world. Our Light is expanded, and the Light in the world increases.

The magic begins as soon as you say *yes* and make that commitment to the sacred journey of coming home to yourself, of being able to rest in the comfort of your own skin. It is a journey of learning, growing, letting go, healing, and evolving. It is not for the fainthearted; it takes courage. It's like signing on for an upgrade in your consciousness, expanding your awareness about yourself and our world.

Allow yourself to come into curiosity and wonder, then witness and lovingly encourage yourself to be honest and candid, follow your Heart, and become your own cheerleader. It's a process. There is no failure, only learning and willingness to course-correct where needed while being kind to yourself and cutting yourself some slack. You have been through a lot in your life, and now you are up to something big and impactful to change your life, remembering who you are. As you grow and evolve, your evolution naturally contributes to change in the world.

Will you settle for your *fate* by doing what you have always done, or will you create your *destiny* by exploring who you are at your core, seeing what you are truly made of—becoming who you came here to be and doing what you came here to do?

You can transform your gifts of sensitivity, your life experiences—the triumphs and the pain and suffering—into a higher purpose. You have been through a particular set of life circumstances and experiences that come together perfectly to shape who you are now, poised for the next level of becoming who you came here to be.

Don't let your past define you but use it as a springboard into a whole new reality for yourself and all of us. It's time to reveal your gifts and hone your wisdom, using them to deeply understand others in circumstances like ones you have been through.

You, as a healed presence, are uniquely positioned to bring a message of hope and ways of support that truly help others. Wherever you are currently is perfect for beginning the journey of coming home to yourself, healing and balancing your body and mind, and exploring your spiritual aspects—that which you truly are at your essence. That's when the whole game will change in your personal world and beyond. Your intuition and multisensory capacities and your uniqueness will become your new normal. You will become who you were meant to be, unfettered by labels, old stories, self-judgements, and self-recriminations.

If you relate to being a sensitive, intuitive, creative, visionary, or dreamer, you have probably had a hard time with trying to fit into the *normal* label. Because you are not. You are not meant to fit in. You are meant to stand out and be yourself. What if being *you* is the greatest gift you could bring to the world?

Key themes to learn from and integrate are *connection*, *conscious choice,* and *reverence* for all life.

Connection

We have been conditioned and distracted into disconnection not only from ourselves—our feelings and our bodies—but also from Mother Nature and a higher power: Source, Creator, Divine, God, Spirit, or whatever name you are comfortable with. The name doesn't matter as long as your Heart's intent is aligned with goodness. Without this deep connection to ourselves, Spirit, and others, life becomes meaningless. We can never grasp who we are and why we are here.

It's essential for our personal and collective future that we reconnect to ourselves, so we can:

- Learn and embrace who we are at the deepest levels
- Connect with our feelings to understand ourselves more deeply
- Connect with our bodies to learn their secrets and how to keep them healthy and happy
- Connect with Nature, be open to her healing qualities, and be inspired by and grounded in her beauty
- Connect with a Higher Intelligence, Creator, Divine through our Heart's intent
- Connect with each other to see the commonality of our struggles and our triumphs
- Celebrate the differences and uniqueness that we each bring

Paradoxically, we can never be disconnected because everything is interconnected, but we can be disconnected from our awareness of it and our experience of it.

Conscious Choice

There are consequences for every choice you make; every action you take has an impact internally and externally. Even not making a choice is a choice. Your choices can lead you to greater or lesser happiness, ease, health, clarity and understanding, or to more confusion with extra obstacles in your way. Many of us often make choices from our unconscious mind through habit and lack of awareness. Many do not realise that choice is always present.

To foster a deeper awareness of yourself and generate more power to effect change, it is critical that you begin to make conscious choices in every decision. It's like training, exercising a new muscle. It may not happen overnight, but with intent, practice, patience, and kindness, you can bring balance and overcome some of the more unconscious choices you may have made in the past that were not helpful. Choosing to learn from the past and present to build awareness of what serves you—your health and wellbeing—and what does not will bring you into greater alignment with knowing and becoming your True Self.

Reverence for All Life

All life is sacred and deserves respect. There is a Divine essence that flows through everything that connects us all to each other, to Nature, and to the Cosmos. Everything impacts everything else. Everything is frequency. When we choose to see Life through the sacred lens of wholeness and beauty everywhere, we change our reality. We are reweaving the sacred back into our everyday lives and Mother Earth. The Sacred Feminine in all of us arises.

Everyone—and everything—has a unique frequency, and that vibration impacts and influences everything else. Frequency is an energy signature, a vibe. There are lower vibes and higher vibes that can affect you without your awareness.

For example, elevated emotions, organic fresh food, and being in Nature create higher frequencies in your body that can help you feel good. Anger, resentment, processed fast food, and desecrated Nature have lower frequencies and can make you less resourceful. When you begin to notice the difference in how these frequencies feel in your body, you will gain more understanding of what serves you and what does not.

You can then make better choices. Ask yourself: Is it a warm, expansive, delicious feeling? Or heavy and restrictive in your body? Where do you feel it in your body? Make a note so you can build a data base.

Each of us is a divine spark of the Creator, a fractal of the whole. Gregg Braden, scientist, author, and thought leader, has popularised the contemporary definition of Divinity as our ability to overcome any perceived human limitations.

What if our Divinity could help us overcome fear as we align ourselves with something greater than ourselves? As we learn, grow, and evolve, we lift our human nature to be embraced by our Divine nature, thus becoming healed and whole. This lift enables us to more easily express our kindness, compassion, and love for ourselves and the world. I believe those expressions are the true nature of humanity; however, we have been conditioned to believe that we are separate from our Divine nature.

Divinity is a word used by religions as well for their purposes. It is not an exclusive thing; it is innate in all of us.

What One Person Can Do

Never underestimate what the power of one person can do to create change. Learning new skills and practices can empower you to create a different outcome for yourself. These skills can then offer a new perspective on what's possible in the world when there is a shift in thinking and an understanding of how that shift contributes to different ways of living, being, and doing in the world.

When you choose to live your life differently—more in alignment with who you came here to be, your authentic self—it affects everyone around you, and the ripple effects reverberate around the world. You lift your vibration and the world lifts.

Be aware that it could make other people around you a bit uncomfortable for a while. Be kind and follow your heart. With other like-minded, like-hearted people, we combine and contribute to creating a whole new reality based on respect, kindness, and sustainability. This new reality needs your willingness to participate, explore, be curious, be open to different information, play, and be a fierce advocate for becoming the best version of yourself.

This book touches upon what has gone wrong: how our health, our sanity, and our knowingness has been hijacked to create a dependent, controlled, over-consuming, over-polluting, sick society. In these pages, I address the physical, emotional, mental, and spiritual aspects of ourselves and explain their function and purpose in creating a healthy relationship with those aspects. I also share the tools that will help bring them into greater balance so that our true nature, our True Self— that has always been present but hidden underneath labels, old stories, and perceived limitations—can be revealed.

I offer simple, practical, life-changing tools of dynamic self-care principles to build awareness and understanding of the genius of your body, to harness the gifts of your mind and emotions, to connect with your authentic self, and to contribute to greater change in the world: one person, one family, one community at a time.

This is a journey to Self and requires a willingness to commit to yourself, learn new skills, course-correct where necessary, be kind to yourself, and celebrate any wins and new learnings.

I invite you to embrace the following as possibilities for changing your life:

- Self-acceptance
- Self-compassion
- Self-responsibility
- Self-respect
- Forgiveness of self
- Self-appreciation
- Self-love

I recommend that you keep a dedicated journal to record insights about your contemplations at any time and whenever you have *aha* moments. Journalling is a powerful tool I encourage you to try as it allows the mind to explore an idea more thoroughly while simultaneously allowing it to release holding all the details—because your mind can trust that its thoughts are now recorded. You will discover rewards as you re-read your entries and track your progress from the beginning through expanding your awareness. Finally, you will see where you land by the end of the book. The journey will continue way beyond reading these pages.

You will grow a new awareness of self, ground yourself, and try on new perspectives, worldviews, and understandings. You will also cultivate a new sense of self as you shed the old with gratitude for how it may have served you in the past.

I hope the information in this book sparks your curiosity and resonates with your Heart—with your knowingness of what's possible for you and what's possible in the world. Some of what I share may be confronting, but I ask that you hold everything loosely, check it out, look for clues, and then decide what resonates and what does not at this time. Consider skipping a chapter and revisiting when ready.

I look forward to walking with you—encouraging, supporting, and celebrating you—through the different sections and exercises, one step at a time, to transform your life into what you desire and deep down, know you deserve.

CHAPTER 1

Who Am I to Tell This Story?

Being Different

For years, I wondered if anyone else out there could see the insanity that was unfolding on this planet. Simple common sense receded into the background, respect for each other and the environment became obsolete, and we were entrained into a new model of complexity, sophistication, and progress at any cost. Success became about how much wealth we could accumulate.

I felt like a lone voice: different, odd. In an effort to fit in with the reality of others, I consciously quietened my own voice and hid aspects of myself that society found undesirable at the time. I did that for years until I realised that I no longer wished to express only part of myself. I wanted more and needed to be the full expression of who I am. I am a work in progress.

I describe myself as a sensitive, intuitive, empath, truth-seeker, and visionary. The world has not been a safe place to express those things too openly. Times are different now, and the world needs the different thinkers to create a new vision and new systems for humanity to move forward.

In the last five to ten years, I have experienced totally different conversations. Is there anyone who cannot see the madness that has been unleashed? People from all walks of life are waking up to the fact that the system is deeply flawed; it is full of injustices, inequities, and unsustainable practices. We have had our freedoms hijacked, our perceptions manipulated, and our planet polluted.

I've been watching the world for some decades and have witnessed a startling decline in so many areas of our world:

- Our physical health with rising statistics in disease and death
- Mental health issues increasing at an alarming rate
- Our ability to think critically against official narratives
- Morality in our political system and business culture
- Education standards and curriculum
- Fairness in our financial and legal systems

These declines—together with modern agricultural practices using chemicals, out of sync with natural environments, limiting our ability to grow healthy, untainted food—are leading to degraded soils and water systems and diminishing habitats with a corresponding alarming increase in extinction rates of species. All of this, of course, impacts human health as we are eating, drinking, and breathing poisoned food, water, and air.

Fear-Based Reality

I could see as a collective, we were becoming deeply entangled in a fear-based reality immersed in scarcity, materialism, competition, and never-ending debt. This progress-and-profit at any cost mentality has led to unhealthy, unsustainable practices in all sectors with most of humanity and Planet Earth suffering as a consequence.

As I travelled deeply down the rabbit holes, my distress compounded. I felt so much anger, disgust, and betrayal. To make things worse, there was no one to share my awareness with. Nobody else in my world at the time could see what I saw or understand it, and they really didn't want to know. I felt so isolated and alone.

By various means over decades and centuries, we have become so disconnected from ourselves, our bodies, Mother Nature, and a Higher Intelligence that our world has become detached, distorted, polarised, chaotic, and confusing. I wonder if we have grown fatigued and worn down by the back-to-back crises over many years and have outsourced our thinking, problem-solving, and planning to those in positions of power.

It's really no wonder, with crises on every front—wars, inflation, natural disasters, food shortages, floods, fires, droughts—that we have been overwhelmed. We are living in times of rapid change, 24/7 surveillance, perceived extensive deterioration of societal values, endless distractions on a plethora of devices, and mainstream media shouting fear-filled messages at us.

Have we unwittingly agreed to whatever is being said and followed along, allowing more and more interference in our lives? Who has the time and energy to discover differently? Are we agreeing to hand over our God-given freedoms and sovereignty in exchange for the illusion of security and safety—breadcrumbs from those who believe they are our rulers?

I believe Benjamin Franklin said something like those who trade their freedoms for the illusion of safety and security receive neither.

I invite you to be curious and open and remind yourself that as you and many others begin to discover and share information, we are together poking holes in the current reality and creating space for what is to come.

The illusions are becoming more visible, breaking apart as more and more people are waking up, turning away from mainstream media, separation tactics, control and misuse of power, and turning to alternative sources of information. Many are now on the search for truth, both in their inner world and our outer world.

Please check the Resources list in the back of this book as a starting point.

A New Roadmap for Humanity

I wondered how I might contribute to navigating our way through these dark, confusing times and shine a light on a path that leads to a whole new reality, rooted in connectedness, kindness, and compassion for ourselves and each other—with Nature and the Divine. I hope to contribute to a roadmap for humanity so we may make it through these transitional times as empowered as possible.

There are many things we can do for ourselves to restore some sense of calm and hope as we move forward to strengthen ourselves and understand what is happening in the world and how to create the best life possible as we navigate new territory.

Now is the time for personal and planetary healing. As we become a healed presence on this planet, we can affect change more rapidly to co-create a fairer, kinder, sustainable world. The world is in desperate need of Heart-centred leaders in our personal and collective lives.

Do you hear the calling?

Imagine for a moment a world where we all thrive in healthy communities in which everyone is respected: our rich cultures, our individuality and uniqueness, and our personal and collective choices, with no harm being caused to ourselves and others.

How can we use our intelligence and intuition, skills and talents, and our conscious choices and actions to bring this new world closer to fruition?

The Evolution of Consciousness

The idea for sharing this knowledge and wisdom gained came to me in 2012. I thought it would be a workshop, but it turned into a book. It has morphed quite a bit from early days in response to what is happening in the world. Things have escalated dramatically and quickly in the last few years. I thought perhaps now people would be ready or desperate enough to find different perspectives and different solutions to what ails our world.

It took many years to see the purpose of my driven research; I couldn't understand at the time why I was gathering all this information. What good purpose could it serve, apart from distracting me from how my life wasn't turning out how I thought it would?

I realised all my life experiences, my decades of research in articles, books, workshops, seminars, summits, and podcasts on everything, can be utilised. I could share what I learned on my journey going down rabbit holes, connecting the dots, and seeing the patterns, using my intuition to see likely scenarios and outcomes.

I had to train myself to handle the devastating truth of what has happened to us as a family of humanity and the forces behind this situation. Most importantly, I needed to be able to extract myself from the pit of despair, disillusionment, and outrage to face the deception and depravity in order to see through the illusions in the world.

Then, I worked diligently to put it all into perspective as part of the Divine Plan for the awakening of humanity and the evolution of our consciousness from separation to unity. If I had not learned that critical part, I would have sunk. I am incredibly sensitive, feeling all the turmoil in the world, and the darkness of tightening control could have left me a quivering mess, useless to be of any help to anyone.

I saw my sensitivity as a weakness for a long time. However, I now see it as a superpower. In a world that is so desensitised to violence and suffering, those of us who can feel and hold all that pain and remain standing—sensing it can be different—are desperately needed.

Unfortunately, it does seem that the vast majority of humanity in its current consciousness is only nudged awake through great devastation. I would have preferred a different way. Perhaps the pressing, squeezing, and stretching that challenging circumstances bring can be utilised to force us to evolve to overcome crises and ignite our vast potential. Seeing all this through the lens of the Divine Plan for unity, consciousness, and liberation of the human race helped me hold steady in the witnessing of atrocities, deception, and injustices that I could not control.

Research

I have spent over thirty years researching human and environmental health and spirituality practices, always looking for what worked—simple, practical ways—to maintain balance and flow in all systems. I obtained information from a lot of different sources, not just one vested interest group. I then became interested in global affairs.

I started to notice recurring themes, and I could see where we were headed as a people. It was not pretty, not normal, and in my view at the time, not necessary. However, we are now in the thick of it, and apparently crises have been necessary to shake us awake to what we have been engaged with. It is crucial to realise we must do things differently to achieve a radically different outcome.

We have been kept in the dark about so much—about our health and understanding, our innate power to create change, to heal ourselves and our world. I have synthesised much of this information—a lot of it based on the principles and practices of the longest living peoples on Earth and the ancient wisdoms of earlier civilisations.

To gain some perspective of what has happened to us—what we have unwittingly co-created and participated in—I share my thoughts about what has been going on in the background. It is more a synopsis than a deep analysis, as I would encourage you to do your own research. There is much information out there provided by good people—doctors, nurses, scientists, lawyers, researchers, whistleblowers, independent film makers, podcasters, mothers and fathers—all motivated to help others know the truth of what has been happening and how to turn these things around, often at great expense to themselves. Many have lost their careers, reputations, financial security, and, in some cases, their lives. But the information keeps coming, nonetheless, by more and more people in the freedom movement. For more information, see the Resources List at the end of the book.

I am always looking for what resonates and what makes sense. I don't claim to have invented or discovered anything new. All I've done is gathered a lot of information, including the truths of the ages, always present, sometimes hidden or obscured. I have been extremely fortunate to have been mentored by brilliant people who have shared their simple, powerful philosophies and practices with me. I checked them out and applied them, and they worked for me. I have now built these truths into the foundation of my life, and they influence me daily.

I developed an insatiable thirst for finding out about why this world wasn't working.

I asked myself:

- Why were people so sick and unhappy, stressed out of their minds?
- Why were our authorities making decisions that poisoned the waters, air, land, and our food system on this planet?
- Why were authorities focussed on just the treatment of illness and not educating to prevent it?
- Why were doctors only trained in disease and very little on health?
- Why was much religious contribution so authoritarian and fear-based, pitting people against each other in the name of a god, when I knew God to be Love?

Blame to Blessings List

After many years of going down rabbit holes, gathering information, feeling the disgust and betrayal of those who were perpetrating what I consider great crimes against humanity, I realised that the anger and desperation I was experiencing were not serving me or the collective. I felt like I was drowning in the muck and mire of the swamp, the negativity engulfing me.

I knew only one thing that could turn it around—sending Light, a practice I learned through my spiritual studies. Martin Luther King, Jr. famously said, *Darkness cannot drive out darkness, and hate cannot overcome hate.* I believe that only Light and Love can accomplish these things.

The Light is always more powerful than the darkness, so I changed my focus from blame to blessings because I understood that this was the only thing that could penetrate the darkness and bring it undone. Immediately, I felt the energetic shift in my body. I was no longer the victim; I was in charge of doing my part to change the situation, to keep myself strong and motivated.

I started blessing the people and institutions I had judged as betraying humanity at the top of my blame list. Shortly after, I started noticing cracks appear in the systems. These cracks have since turned into gaping holes—exposing a lot of deception and corruption—leading to the crumbling and collapse of the old regime that has controlled the world for hundreds of years. For the new to come forward, the old must collapse. We cannot rebuild on faulty foundations.

We have lived under a toxic, authoritarian, patriarchal control system in an artificially constructed, fake matrix world based on our conditioning, perceptions, and beliefs for a long time. Everything has been designed to confuse and disempower us, to make us toe the line and accept the status quo under fear of punishment.

My hope is that this information will help you understand why the world is so dysfunctional and see that much that has happened has been deliberately orchestrated. As we build our awareness, we are gradually letting go of the hold the chaotic drama world of 3-D has had on us. It will lose resonance and will not be able to sustain itself. There is no time for sugarcoating this information. We are in the midst of a massive shift of consciousness for humanity. It's messy, painful, and sometimes horrific as we push through the layers of density we have been immersed in for a long time.

What I know to be true is that we are one family, brothers and sisters, no matter our colour or culture. There is only one Source that created all Life, and it loves *all* of its creation. There is no force greater than this. None.

Healing, Hope, and Wholeness

My deepest desire is to bring hope and inspiration for others to commit to the inner work to heal ourselves physically, emotionally, and mentally to co-create a brilliant awe-inspiring collective future.

There is a lot of work to be done. So much damage has been done to our psyche and our bodies. Belief systems are skewed and distorted. We are continually polarised and separated through the peddling of fear about everything through mainstream media. With focus, intentional work, and collaboration, we can transform and transmute it all, making ourselves and the world whole again—wiser, stronger, happier, and healthier. I have no doubt this will happen. It can happen sooner with your participation. Be curious about what that might look like for you.

There is a huge movement towards freedom, connection, creativity, collaboration, and community around the world. It used to be underground, but now it's more visible and louder than ever. Can you sense it?

As part of the healing process, we need to acknowledge our past, to witness personal and collective hardships and trauma endured, not allowing it to define us but to shape and strengthen us. It is important to feel and express deep reverence for the journeys we have lived through. It has been so hard for so many for so long.

We need to honour the sacred in all life, reconnecting with the Divine. We need to be open and curious, to ask what else is possible for us and our loved ones and for this magnificent family of humanity as we move into the new story of *us*.

In the coming pages, I share my thoughts on what has happened to us in the past to explain why things are so unsupportive of humanity thriving. Then I bring in the bigger picture from different avenues of thought about what could be happening. I also share my relevant life experiences and learnings that I hope will ignite your curiosity, prompt your own memories—the enjoyable ones, acute learning ones, and unresolved ones still calling for your loving attention.

My stories—our stories—reflect what is going on in the world, the inner and outer battles. If we adjust our focus, we will also see inner and outer beauty. I will also share the tools and practices that allowed me to heal my old stories of pain and suffering and create new stories and an awareness of possibilities for greater happiness and health that became the foundation of my life.

CHAPTER 2

How Did We Get Here?

Challenging Times

To better understand where we are and why, we need to know a little more about what has been going on behind the scenes for a very long time. We are living through unprecedented, extraordinary times, never before experienced in recorded history. The world is going through rapid change, and the goal posts we once used to navigate life are in free fall. It looks like the world we have known is falling apart, and it is. Yet, there is also a palpable potency and potential for the new to come forward.

We are caught in a liminal space bridging two realities. The new world is not yet visible to most. The old is coming undone, and the not knowing and uncertainty are creating tension in many people who simply want to return to the old or find a saviour of religious or political stature. Returning to the old is no longer an option; that world is untethered and unravelling.

What if *we* are the solution, the ones we have been waiting for?

What we have been witnessing is the last throes of a dying regime that is refusing to give in without a fight. It has been like an invisible world government influencing every country, setting up institutions that serve their cause, infiltrating every government, cabinet, organisation, agency, and system in politics, finance, education, health, law, energy, military, science, and foreign relations.

These kinds of activities have been going on for centuries behind the scenes, quietly moving the chess pieces around to maintain and enforce the dominant position of power. However, it seems that in the last few years, our rulers and controllers have become more daring and visible, creating an unintended consequence of sparking awareness in many people that something is deeply flawed with our systems.

Influences That Have Shaped Our Society

I will use America as an example, as whatever happens in America affects the rest of the world and is usually duplicated in other countries. In November 1913, a small group of the most powerful men in the United States and the world gathered on a private island off the East Coast of America to draft a plan for a new central bank in the States, which would come to be called the Federal Reserve.

There is a theory—many will call it a conspiracy—that this group of ultra-wealthy banking families came together as a cartel to create a new bank privately owned by them. The official narrative is that it falls under the umbrella of government. Time will reveal the truth. If this theory were true, could it have greatly enriched the top echelon of society and given them enormous power to influence government and, over time, impoverish the rest?

Consider reading *The Creature from Jekyll Island* by G. Edward Griffin if interested. In this age of misinformation and disinformation, it is important to polish up our discernment skills.

The Flexner Report of 1910 was commissioned by the Carnegie Foundation to evaluate medical schools based on scientific rigour and adherence, despite the lack of medical training of Abraham Flexner. After the report was published, the implementation was funded by the Rockefeller organisations, ensuring that schools aligned with pharmaceutical and surgical models became dominant, and those offering alternative training had funding withdrawn (Leister 2025).

This report had profound consequences as about half of all medical schools were closed down, particularly those teaching homeopathy, naturopathy, herbal medicine, and other non-allopathic therapies. Medical schools stopped teaching nutrition, lifestyle, and alternative approaches in psychiatric treatment. These alternatives were considered inadequate, quackery, and unscientific nonsense. They had been accepted as safe and effective medicines for decades in America and other countries—and even favoured by the royal family in the UK. Any competition to the medical model seemed to be ridiculed, censored, demonised, considered anti-science, silenced, and eradicated.

Those same practices of condemnation continue today. I wonder: Is this reform or monopoly? In my view, modern medicine excels at acute responses to accidents, heart attacks, and more, but not chronic disease. Petrochemically derived medication can bring relief but cannot heal an organic body. Our bodies are starving for true nutrition, and our psyche needs an intelligent gentle approach to healing our trauma. Those two things alone would go a long way to improving our health and wellbeing.

Our education system should be about stimulating curiosity, cultivating a love of learning, developing critical thinking skills, and discovering the interests and unique genius of each individual. It seems to me that many schools dampen the imagination and eagerness of children to learn, and instead they promote conformity, obedience, repetition, and standardised tests and offer tedious topics that aren't relevant. This could create a nation of obedient workers, not necessarily critical thinkers.

A 1960s NASA-commissioned study by Dr. George Land found that 98 percent of four to five-year-olds scored as creative geniuses. Follow-up testing on the same children revealed by grade one, their scores had dropped to 30 percent; by high school, only 12 percent tested in this category. They also conducted the same test on a group of adults and found less than 2 percent were creative geniuses (Land 1992).

Could our education system be stifling our creativity and dumbing us down?

Mainstream media has enormous power and influence over the narratives about topics that shape our lives, such as wars, economic policy, and environmental issues. Ownership of these outlets is concentrated into the hands of a few wealthy people, who may be motivated to protect their vested interests. These people could be considered part of the group we often call the *Elite*.

If we consider the word *government*, *govern* means to control and *ment* is derived from *mentis*, meaning the mind. Is the government in the business of mind control? Perhaps we could call it perspective management, which is aided by the mainstream media to broadcast to the masses particular narratives with an inbuilt bias that we call *the news*. The news, in turn, influences our thinking, our opinions, our beliefs about the events.

In my view, we have:

- Governments that rule instead of serve
- Financial systems that make us poor
- Health systems that make us sick
- Education systems that make us ignorant and complacent
- Legal systems that are unfair
- Food systems that grow poisoned, genetically-altered food with little nutritional value
- Mainstream media that manipulates truth or outright lies to serve the official narratives authored by their employers

Dreamspell

It's like we've all been living in a dreamspell, similar to the lead character in *The Truman Show* (Weir 1998). For his whole life, he had been conditioned to believe that his world was all that existed. His beliefs had been shaped by those around him in his family, his culture, and his perceived authority figures. He grew up in a controlled environment that informed his beliefs and behaviours. I think we will discover soon that a contrived worldview has been imposed upon us, and we will see it for the illusion it is—just like in this movie.

Broken Systems

In my view, we are overgoverned and over-lobbied by vested interests that seem to be directing policy for their own profit, not in favour of the people nor the environment on which our lives depend. We are overregulated, over-surveilled, overexploited, over-sanitised, over-poisoned, over-plasticised, overmedicated, over-polluted, overfed and undernourished, underappreciated, and under-expressed. We are more and more stressed about losing our autonomy, health, finances, work, and relationships. We are more worried about the economy, wars, widespread sickness, and government actions—or inactions—than ever before.

Many feel they have limited access to the resources and opportunities to create something different. We need to look outside the box to find different answers, different ways of doing things, to be able to sustain ourselves physically, emotionally, mentally, and spiritually. The old ways are no longer working for us. This is part of the paradigm shift.

As a collective, we are in new territory. Old systems are cracking and crumbling as their dysfunction engulfs them. Scandals of our leaders and high-profile people are revealed daily, and the fabric of life as we have known it is unravelling.

The model of *might is right*—needing to be bigger and more cutthroat to survive, Darwinian model of survival of the strongest that is currently operating—has reigned supreme for some time. I don't believe it is a natural way for people to operate and exchange equal value. We have been conditioned to think, through our financial and business training and cultural narratives, that this model is the only way to prosper.

Get big or get rubbed out and—lo and behold—that is the kind of world we have created. That is the reality presented in our daily dose of hypnosis via media: a world full of drama, chaos, violence, lack, disparity, unfairness, and more. Agreed, they all exist, but I think it distorts our view of others and our world, as there is so much goodness in the world that is not highlighted.

Manipulation and Control

I believe that critical mass has been reached in the desire of most people for a better world: kinder, peaceful, cooperative, sustainable. We need to pierce the veils of illusion and witness what has been going on in the background—how we as the 99 percent have been manipulated and enslaved in a grindstone system that serves the top 1percent. How did we allow that to happen?

Where can we take personal responsibility? Most of us are too tired and stressed to research what has been and is happening. We trusted our authorities to take care of us. That's what they wanted us to think. Imagine how powerful we truly are! They have had to go to extraordinary lengths to dumb us down, make us sick and weak to control us, mostly through poisoning and mind control. We have been manipulated in order to divert us from being able to access our inner power—we're taught that God, Creator, Divine is separate and outside of us—so we would be easier to control through complacency and compliance, helplessness and hopelessness.

We live in a world that essentially has been artificially constructed by shaping our beliefs, behaviours, perspectives, attitudes, and our identities. We could call it a matrix. Many people say *The Matrix* movie is a documentary. Perhaps it is. We could also say that perhaps *Star Wars* and *Star Trek* are soft disclosures.

It is a peculiar part of the elite's *code of honour* to tell us what is coming through *science fiction*. Consider all the movies about wars, pandemics, famines, climate crisis, environmental collapse, alien invasion, political dishonesty, and manipulation. Films normalise those sorts of events in our awareness; therefore, we accept them when they happen because we think they are normal. *Seen that before!* so there is nothing we can do about them.

Could it be possible that many of the ills of the world have been orchestrated? Who would stand to gain?

There has been a battle going on for millennia for control over humanity—our minds and our bodies—to enslave us in a system that is unsustainable and does not serve us. It has mostly been covert, but since 2020 has become visible to those with the eyes to see and the ears to hear. That is when insanity reigned supreme.

We have been steeped in a world filled with dramas, polarisation, isolation, destructive conditioning, distorted mainstream media, and low frequency leaders of lesser integrity so that chaos, confusion, and crises have ruled supreme. The 1 percent at the top of the pyramid have been humanity's controllers for a very long time by peddling endless fear through mainstream media, turmoil, and chaos to weaken us, divide us, and make us compliant to their pre-prepared solutions. They have created authoritarian patriarchal control systems that have been engineered for profit, not service to the people. They work from the rulebook of *divide and conquer*, keeping the masses in fear, creating narratives that frighten and polarise. These methods will no longer work if we are committed to our growth, evolution, and unity. Their tactics will become obsolete like the current ruling power.

What if a lot of promoted fear is *False Evidence Appearing Real?* Fear weakens us and makes us easier to control if we believe the narrative, because we are looking for a solution to ease our worries. Luckily, the government always has a pre-prepared solution. We are herded into particular directions through a tried and very tested method, a sophisticated tool of persuasion:

Problem > Reaction > Solution

First, powers that be create a *solution* that is needed to achieve desired objectives, then a problem is created, or an existing one is exploited, allowing people to work themselves into a frenzy, demanding a solution. They repeat the story over and over with specific emotive language on media, then leak rumours from a *trusted source* of the preferred solution that sounds like a panacea to the problem. Then, a seemingly benevolent power provides the solution they wanted to instigate all along. It is a slick, sophisticated, mostly-hidden method used for control and achieving certain goals.

In this tried-and-trusted formula, there is no room for messengers with a different perspective that does not fit the mainstream narrative. They are ridiculed and hounded, their reputation dismantled, no matter how esteemed they were before the dissenting message. Sometimes, the transgression is as innocuous as a different suggestion or approach to the problem, or questioning the remedy offered. These *offenses* are enough to be silenced.

Our rulers and controllers have infiltrated and captured just about every government and organisation, including our regulatory agencies, which now represent the very industry they should be regulating. We have been surveilled, studied, and experimented on for decades to understand how to shape our perspectives, to create a narrative that would polarise our opinions and create divisions in society.

It seems they have weaponised our very humanness through invoking our compassion and inclusive nature to turn us against each other by making us choose artificially produced sides. They have used an incredibly sophisticated system of manipulation that not many could see. It is important to rise above it all, to gain altitude, and see events from a higher perspective.

Then we can see the tawdry scenery, the old men pulling the levers behind the curtains, just like Dorothy and companions experienced in *The Wizard of Oz*.

Mind Control

Psyops, or psychological operations, are mental manipulations or mind control that has been used to direct us into specific perspectives that will inform the choices and decisions we make to fit others' agendas in order to have the desired *obvious solution* accepted. Repetitive content and specific verbalisations are used to cast the spell to entrain us into a certain way of thinking—certain perspectives or points of view—to direct us into a particular response and action, a form of perspective management or manipulation. It is subtle, yet powerful, and not obvious to many. But people are now waking up to the great deception.

Propaganda is real. Once you see the patterns, you are better prepared for the next time. I believe we are being controlled and manipulated from unseen forces as described by Edward Bernays in his book *Propaganda*:

The conscious and intelligent manipulation of the organized habits and opinions of the masses are an important element in democratic society. Those who manipulate this unseen mechanism of society constitute an invisible government, which is the true ruling power of our country (Bernays 1928).

We're now seeing more clearly the worst crimes committed against humanity being exposed: orchestrated provocation of wars, sex trafficking, and the deliberate poisoning of our food, our bodies, and our waters, air, and land. The level of corruption, fraud, greed, and deception is deep and wide and systemic. The extent could be a shock to many people.

I offer a possible example that may seem exaggerated. Hopefully, it is. Let's say those who are accustomed to wielding power with little or no opposition devise a daring new scheme of exceptional control over the population to greater depth, height, and width than ever before. An absolutely audacious proposal requires absolute audacious deception to get to the desired solution. They start with a little lie, then another, and they build twists and turns into it, adding restrictions so people cannot exercise their freedom to make their own choices. The messages are repeatedly broadcast worldwide by the chief experts on the project through mainstream media owned by the biggest stakeholders. The broadcasts are repetitive to drill the message into the subconscious to make sure people's perspectives align with the desired solution.

As the lies start to grow bigger and bigger and more and more obvious to some, dissenters or naysayers who question and do not comply with the official narrative are shamed, blamed, ridiculed, and called irresponsible for stepping out of the perceived majority mentality. Online censoring and deplatforming of those offering alternative information to the mainstream narrative becomes rampant. It becomes a badge of honour to be deplatformed, blocked, or censored because it means they are speaking Truth and must be silenced so as not to weaken the mainstream narrative.

There is a lot of evidence gathering, and many survivors and whistleblowers are willing to share their experience that mind control has not only been sanctioned by our governments, but they have also provided funding to tech giants, who have employed surveillance of us as consumers of social media for years, to harvest and share our data so it can be utilised by our intelligence and security agencies.

Data brokering is an incredibly lucrative business in which our personal data is collected and sold, all without our willing consent. They spy on us to learn our patterns of thinking, interests, and likes and dislikes under the pretence that they want to serve us with marketing material that may interest us. All the while, they are harvesting data to store, share, and sell.

This may sound like conspiracy theories. That's okay. Hold it loosely. Evidence will come out to prove or disprove it in the future.

Climate Change and Pollution

We are in a period of climate extremes, which has created much change and crisis in different areas. I know I am going against conventional beliefs, but I do not believe that humans are solely responsible for global warming (Braden 2020). The computer models used to support climate crisis do not go back far enough in time before the industrial age to show there is a true crisis. Many of the earlier projections did not come true (Braden 2020).

There are natural cycles over thousands of years in which temperatures have been higher than they are now and also much colder. Data is collected from ice core samples from the poles. The cycles of the sun—solar maximum and solar minimum—play a big part in those cycles. There are other factors as well. Carbon is the building block of all life on Earth. I do not believe it is a pollutant (Gamble 2018).

I do believe that humans are responsible for the levels of pollution of our land, rivers, oceans, and skies. The clear felling of vegetation over vast swathes of the planet affects the microclimate, the health of soils, the taking up of carbon, and the contribution of oxygen to the atmosphere. The corporations manufacturing pollutive chemicals and the global mega corporations that own them have many lobbyists backed by big money to incentivize governments to create policies that can facilitate circumventing regulations, dumping waste, and ignoring their responsibility to clean up their mess. In an ideal world, it would be better not to create it in the first place by employing effective assessment reviews, monitoring, and reporting at every stage.

We can all make a difference and turn the tide by withdrawing as much as possible from the systems that pollute our environment, making different choices in what we purchase and in what we engage.

Change Is Here

The storm is here. Systems are breaking down and disasters are everywhere, but crisis can also bring opportunity for change and enormous growth on all levels. Chaos always precedes evolution; it is the impetus from *breakdown* to *breakthrough*. We are in the midst of an evolutionary leap in the consciousness of humankind, in understanding who we are and what we are capable of.

The journey can be ugly, messy, frightening, painful, lonely, and confusing, yet liberating and empowering also. We continue as something within us says a more beautiful, kinder world is possible. We must navigate these turbulent times to help co-create a new Earth. The process has begun.

The more of us who join in, the quicker change will happen. Know that you are not alone. There are many of us around the globe finding each other, joining resources, building communities.

As Einstein famously said, we cannot solve the problems of the world from the level of thinking that created them in the first place. The consciousness of many of our political and business leaders—high profile or behind the scenes—is not one that seeks to serve the people and planet, but rather its own interests.

Many modern leaders represent the old model, authoritarian leadership style—cunning intellect, domineering, and centralised—with an acute lack of transparency, accountability, and connection to the people or their real needs. They are held accountable only to profit margins and power. Scarcity, competition, and debt-based economic models lend themselves well to maintaining power.

However, all is not lost. Hope springs eternal in my Heart. Every day, I see wonderful people doing wonderful things in the world. Deep in the core of my being, I know we've got this, that humanity triumphs over dire adversity. Each person has a responsibility to educate themselves and play their part in this paradigm shift in whatever way feels right for them.

Buckminster Fuller, a brilliant thought leader and futurist once said something like: *If you want to change the system, a revolution is not needed, just build a new model and the old will become obsolete* (Buckminster Fuller Institute 2024). I believe that is what is happening now. Many communities with an Earth-based focus are gathering, building, and sharing resources to create a slower, more meaningful, connected lifestyle.

There are many independent podcasters (see Resources) who are interviewing amazing people with incredible information to share with us because mainstream media will not cover these topics. These media outlets dismiss and silence anyone and anything that challenges the accepted official narrative that their controllers and employers direct them to broadcast.

Never again will we allow governments and corporations to take control over our lives, destroy the environment, diminish our dignity, or scatter family values to the four winds. Together—individually and collectively—we will dream and build a new viable future that's beautiful and wholesome, respectful, and cooperative, and we will source from that place of vision and strength to pull us through.

CHAPTER 3

Cycles of Change

There was a lot of hype about the end of the world in 2012, based on an interpretation of the Mayan Calendar that clearly showed the end of a cycle when things would break down—not necessarily end—to begin another roughly 5,000-year cycle. Five of these cycles compose a longer cycle of nearly 26,000 years called the Precession of the Equinoxes.

Earth's axis wobbles slowly like a spinning top and takes about 26,000 years to complete one revolution of this wobbling cycle. It is a gradual rotation of the pattern of stars around the ecliptic axis. I believe this is where our zodiac constellations are seen. We are closing one cycle and beginning a new 26,000-year cycle of potential expansion and upliftment.

The Kali Yuga of Hindu tradition is said to be the last of four ages from the pinnacle of enlightenment, descending into the depths of deception, greed, immorality, and injustice. This age is the time we have experienced and are moving through now. Bibhu Dev Misra, after years of extensive research, believes the end of that age could be as soon as March 2025 (Dev Misra

2023). Then, we move into an ascending cycle. The whole cycle of four ages is roughly 26,000 years, also aligned with the Precession of Equinoxes.

Astrologically, we are also moving from the Age of Pisces, which is about individually exploring ourselves as spiritual beings and releasing illusions of separation to embrace unity consciousness. We are on the threshold of the Age of Aquarius, which focuses on more of a *we* consciousness while maintaining our individuality.

These Age cycles are over 2000 years long. There are twelve zodiac signs, and one revolution through them takes roughly 25–26,000 years, similar to the Precession cycle. This shift of the ages is of epic proportions, and there is a lot at stake. This period is when civilisations may end, unless they choose to change and build a new model.

Approximately every 12,000 years—in the Ages of Leo and Aquarius—our solar system enters what is called the Photon Belt, sometimes called the Rings of Alycone, in our galaxy. Photons are microscopic particles of Light. Light has been considered *information* by many throughout our history. When we shine the Light into the darkness, we see what is there, and we see further because we have more information.

We are being inundated with Light, with information to upgrade our awareness, lift our consciousness, to see through the illusions of this world, and to return to our knowing, living in harmony with Nature and each other. I believe the majority of people on Earth want peace. It's only our leaders and their controllers that want war, conquest, and control. And profit. Not for much longer! We are disengaging from that vision and creating a new one. We divert our energy from what we don't want to create to what we do want.

Many cultures around the world have prophesied that there would be a paradigm shift for humanity in these times. They expect major changes in our world will occur. Many of us have sensed something big has been coming for a long time, and we have been waiting.

We are now in this time of great change. Nothing can stop it unfolding. We are living in challenging times, experiencing an upgrade in our understanding of who we are, why we are here, and where we came from. All this rapid change could appear frightening to many people. The more we know ourselves, the better we can navigate the road ahead.

So much mystery and magic about our cosmological story is yet to be revealed in the coming years, as well as our history on Earth. Much of what we have been taught is now seen as incomplete, inaccurate, and in some places, possibly pure fabrication. New evidence being found around the world does not support the old theories of human evolution we have accepted as truth. According to Gregg Braden, the evidence supports plant and animal evolution, but not human (Braden 2017). These *anomalies* present a very different story of us, perhaps one of Divine intention and purpose.

Ancient Civilisations

Researchers and scientists are currently uncovering ancient civilisations that had skills and abilities we do not have today. There are enormous structures, thousands of years old, built by earlier civilisations, that our technology cannot duplicate. Hundreds, if not thousands, of pyramids exist around the world, and we have been told they were built by slaves with rocks and ropes. Research continues to explore the mysteries of pyramid-building using advanced technologies, but scientists are edging closer and closer by using ancient and timeless technologies, such as sound frequency, that people in ancient times had knowledge of and access to.

I invite you to check out the Gaia website (Gaia.com), which offers many series with scientists of different disciplines piecing together a new story of our origins.

The Feminine and Masculine Out of Balance

The body of Mother Earth is a representation of the Divine Feminine—the Divine Mother—and has been subjected to exploitation, extractive practices, desecration, and decimation in so many places. Nature in the dictionary is clearly defined as separate from people in order to justify many rapacious activities.

We are undoubtedly a part of Nature; our very bodies are made from the elements of the earth. Our food is grown in the earth; our shelter is provided by Nature. We naturally feel good in Nature—quieter, calmer—as we inhale more oxygen and enjoy birdsong and sunshine. Its beauty and wonder are sources of inspiration for us.

We could not exist without Nature. She could survive without us, but I think she would be lonely. We had a symbiotic relationship with her in the past. She would provide abundantly for us, and we would honour, respect, and take care of her through our custodial responsibilities. We have strayed far from the original intent.

Many of the Indigenous peoples of the world who understood and fulfilled the role of custodians have been divided, conquered, silenced, poisoned, disempowered, and separated from their culture, country, stories, and language. Many have languished in the world of their dominant culture through the loss of meaning in their lives and the stories of who they have been as a people.

I believe this knowing and connection is returning, especially with younger generations.

In a world where the Divine Feminine has been brutally suppressed and the Sacred Masculine has been severely distorted, what hope have we had of creating a happy, healthy, functioning humanity and a sustainable, abundant world?

The Inquisition was set up by the Roman Catholic Church to try and convict people who challenged their teachings. This tribunal created a reign of terror and brutality that lasted for at least 400 years from the fourteenth to eighteenth centuries. It was even called the *Holy* Inquisition, but there is no holiness in such widespread taking of human life throughout Europe and beyond for the crime of having ideas that challenged the doctrine of the Catholic Church.

This was the time of the witch hunts targeting women healers who used herbs to heal wounds and diseases and safely delivered babies into the world—therefore, seen as witch magic. Many men were also victims. That violence and resulting trauma is in our genetic makeup. We do not have to have been burnt at the stake to be affected by violence. Nobody is untouched by trauma; the perpetrators, victims, and onlookers are all affected.

The Sacred Masculine has been impacted by all the wars that have been fought and endured with unthinkable terrors. Sadly, they are still happening. Think of Hollywood movies with their macho, remote, emotionally-devoid heroes taking out lives here, there, and everywhere to *win* the day. The disrespect for all life and harmony is palpable.

Many programs on TV are programmed to tell-a-vision about death, doom and gloom, disrespect, and revenge. This tone becomes normalised in our culture. What happened to the shows that explored kind, loving families and healthy relationships in which laughter was a shared experience and not at someone else's expense?

Exercise

If you consider that Feminine qualities embody the intuitive, reflective, flowing, collaborative, creative, nurturing, and inner-focussed thinking and the Masculine encompasses strategic, linear, competitive, outward-focused thinking, ask yourself these questions and journal about any sights you have:

- What can I do differently to support myself to balance the Feminine and Masculine energies within me and in my relationships?
- Which part do I think needs encouragement or calming?
- How can I express both aspects in my personality in respectful ways that feel authentic and enhance my life?

Colonisation

Think of the demoralisation and near decimation of the indigenous peoples of many lands in the name of religion and colonisation. Colonisation affects all of us. All these traumas are our ancestral inheritance and encoded in our DNA. Trauma weakens our DNA and makes us susceptible to disease. These wounds can be healed if we choose to do inner work with kindness as outlined in the Tools of Consciousness in Chapter 7.

Lost Our Way

We are here at such a pivotal time on Planet Earth. Humanity has lost its way, forgotten who we are, not knowing or understanding our skills and capacities for brilliance and genius, innovation, creativity, connection, and collaboration. We have been endlessly distracted by events, infotainment, and hypnotic devices, conditioned to believe we are separate from Nature and Creator. We live in a materialistic competitive dog-eat-dog world of scarcity for most and obscene wealth for a few, and we accept that this is our lot in life.

The disrespect for our environment and our bodies, ignoring common sense, and believing specifically fashioned narratives about ourselves and our world have their consequences. They have created and constructed a world of extreme disparity and polarity: the powerful and the seeming powerless, the *haves* and *have-nots*.

This is the biggest shift for humanity in its evolution: to understand the powerful beings that we truly are. We are right in the midst of this shift of paradigms from the old world to the new. The old is crumbling before our eyes, and the new is not quite visible to most yet. It's like straddling two worlds, and it's uncomfortable, not quite *there* and not yet *here*.

New Systems

New dynamic systems are being created and organised by people at the grassroots level, where true sustainable change is birthed. From farmers of regenerative agriculture that respect Mother Nature's cycles; law experts exploring freedom to enlightened doctors and natural medicine practitioners; from biologists, soil scientists, neuroscientists to chefs and independent student-focussed teachers; from young enthusiastic entrepreneurs to the elders coming forward to share their experiences, knowledge, and wisdom—all are contributing to a different outcome for our world.

I believe we all have gifts and talents and genius that are unique to us and, combined with our own life experiences, are waiting to be tapped, developed, and expressed into the world. In times to come, we will move towards more ethical, conscious business operations in which cooperation and collaboration will be the modus operandi. This shift will allow the talents and skills of individuals to be utilised for the greater good of the collective.

What if the degree to which the world is not working is directly related to the degree to which we have not yet developed our potentials? We need out-of-the-box thinking! We need different thinkers to take a quantum leap of faith into believing that all our talents and resources are needed now in whatever context is calling us forward to contribute.

There is a whole new opportunity now to change the trajectory of this world from seeming disaster and possible annihilation to one of thriving communities built on trust, a common vision towards cooperation, collaboration, and true sustainability. We need different tools to empower us to take back the driver's seat in our own lives, to make some different choices to create different outcomes for ourselves and the planet.

If we don't, nothing will change, and the status quo will remain, and things will become more extreme.

Is that even possible? Unfortunately yes, but the chances are diminishing.

What will it take for us all to assume personal responsibility for what we have contributed with our deliberately orchestrated ignorance and complacency and to understand and own that we are powerful creators? We can create something different, something so good and so powerful it becomes unstoppable. The process has already begun. The only negotiable I see is *how soon*. And that depends on who and how many choose to become involved in the greatest awakening unfurling on this planet.

There is a whole new reality being created alongside this one, based on truth and freedom. We are realising that we are all interconnected, and everything impacts on everything else. What we do to ourselves, we do to each other, and, in turn, our actions impact everyone and our planet. It may not be obvious to some, but every action, every thought has a ripple effect that impacts all of us.

Are our actions, our thoughts, our beliefs, our stories contributing to a more sustainable, healthy, more joyful world— or to maintain the status quo? The results lie on a continuum with a constant sliding scale, but I sense the *weight* is shifting to a whole new perspective on life: who we are and what we are capable of. It's choice time.

As a collective, we are being invited into the greatest possibility to move from a fear-based reality of separation, lack, competition, and materialism to one rooted in kindness, respect, compassion, connection, creativity, and collaboration. It's a huge undertaking. We all have a part to play in the turning of the wheel, and we are all needed.

A New Model of Leadership

A different model of leadership is needed, one more aligned to the Feminine power model of vision, cooperation, and collaboration. This model of sourcing from within, aligning with a higher purpose will replace the old out-of-date corrupt patriarchal power model of control, authority, competition, and aggression. A new balance is being created as both Feminine and Masculine qualities are being recognised and honoured as equal and different. Both are absolutely essential to moving forward in this world.

It's clearly time for a new way of living and of being in relationship with all life. The level of change required will not happen if we sit by and do nothing. If we stay in our comfort zone, which is fast disappearing, we won't grow, and we will never know what we are capable of. Then, the opportunity to create a fair sustainable new Earth could be delayed.

Choice

It is important to find simple basic tools to empower yourself to choose differently, to create more harmony, peace, vitality, and energy in your life. Your quality of life depends on it. Do you want to simply survive, or do you want to thrive? If there were no perceived obstacles in your life, what would you choose for yourself? What kind of life would you create and generate for yourself, others, and our future generations?

Choosing to live your life differently from before creates more possibilities, more choices, and more opportunities. You can put yourself in a whole new groove and upgrade to a magnificent contribution to yourself, others, and the world.

We are multifaceted beings with an enormous capacity for change and growth in our awareness; therefore, we have the ability to take action to create a healthier, happier, sustainable future for ourselves and the generations to come.

Make the different choices needed to create a different kind of life for yourself and a different reality in the world. Educate yourself, which will involve unlearning a lot of what you thought was true. Be open, hold everything loosely, seek out different information from non-mainstream sources, cross reference, and see what resonates for you as you build a new foundation for your life. There is no need to believe anything I say. I am sharing my opinions based on my years of research and life experiences. Always do your own research. I will provide suggested resources at the end of book.

Have the Courage to Trust Your Heart

I am a simple country girl who has now lived in a city for most of my life, but my Heart remains country. I recall my grandmother used to say *the truth is always simple.* I don't know that I fully understood it then, but it resonated with me, and that's been a guiding principle in my life. I realised that even if my mind didn't understand what was for my highest good, my Heart, that higher part of consciousness, knew it and aligned with it. Also, I have learned that my Heart is my trusted barometer for Truth in my life.

It takes a lot of courage to leave behind what we've always known, as dysfunctional and unsustainable as it has been for a long time. As the old era disintegrates before our very eyes, it is critical we learn new skills and practices to master our energies. The last few years of heightened turmoil has created much fear and uncertainty, which has traumatised all of us, and the intensity is rapidly rising.

We need to distance ourselves from the hold the 3-D level world has had on us, filled with dramas, polarisation, isolation, destructive conditioning, distorted mainstream media, and low integrity leaders—a world in which chaos, confusion, and crises have ruled supreme. Eventually, as we learn to focus on what we do want rather than what we do not want, the old fear-based reality will lose resonance and will not be able to sustain itself because enough people will wake up to the great deception and choose differently.

This is the great awakening that some people call *ascension*. Many of us are already letting go, lifting our focus, raising our vibes, and, therefore, making progress traversing this part of the journey that looks a lot like nightmare alley.

We must balance the bad news with our good intentions and positive focus and then take inspired actions to forge a new path ahead.

Change

What if we could change the lens through which we have seen the world and consider that maybe everything is serving to wake us up from the generational hypnotic trance we have been immersed in for decades, centuries, and maybe longer so we can clearly see what we have been engaged with, participated in, and unwittingly helped to perpetuate. What are we personally and collectively no longer willing to tolerate, no longer willing to turn away from and pretend it's not happening?

Change always begins from the inside out. There is no bypassing the inner work. I guarantee you will be a different person—happier, healthier, clearer—if you focus on this sacred work. There will never be peace in the outer world unless we choose peace inside ourselves first. We must heal the inner battles that perpetuate our suffering. We can become the calm centre in the storm encircling us.

CHAPTER 4

My Learning and Growth Journey

Growing Up

I have always had a deep connection to Nature; it is restorative for me. It can calm me down, yet energise me, and gives me a sense of freedom that everything is alright in my world. I was also sensitive to others and their feelings. Being so sensitive often felt a burden, feeling the deep, overwhelming emotions I didn't understand at the time. Those feelings were just another inconvenient thing to control, and I believed I mustn't express them too much, especially unhappy or angry ones.

I was basically a quiet, reserved child, as my teachers described me. I did have occasional outbursts at home if I considered something was unfair. Mostly, I was just curious and wanted to know why things were the way they were.

I remember living on a farm as a small child in the 1950s—the smell of the sweet earth my father held in his hands as he squatted next to me and extended his hands under my nose. He put some in my tiny hands to feel the texture as it clumped and then fell to the ground. It was rich with humus, organic matter from the pea crop he had ploughed into the ground to allow the nitrogen and other nutrients to return to the soil, feeding the next crop he would plant.

He understood the cycles of Nature and how to work with them to serve the health of the soil, so Nature could serve our health. It was an important lesson I never forgot: Look after Mother Nature, work with her natural cycles and what will support her fertility, so she can provide for our needs.

I spent a lot of my early childhood wandering the farm alone, as my older siblings were at school. I was never lonely. I would visit my favourite places: the rocky limestone outcrop, the grove of melaleuca trees. Sometimes, I made my own crop circles in the middle of a field of grain. I folded down the still green stalks and padded out a circle that fit me lying down so I could view the beautiful ever-changing clouds as Creator entertained me and revealed its mystery.

Crop Dusting

The first notion I had that something was not right in my world was when crop dusting began in our area. I was still quite young and didn't know what it was, but as the smell entered my nostrils, I felt deep in my body it was not good. In fact, I felt it was harmful to all life. I remember my mother grabbing the washing off the clothesline and moving us both inside quickly and then rapidly closing all the windows. I felt her anxiety and wondered.

Nobody asked questions in those days. We accepted this was somehow progress, and we believed we should be grateful for this marvellous technology that combined with the application of synthetic, imbalanced fertilisers and was going to make farming easier and more productive. We never realised the impact it would have on our health and that of the soil and planet. Years later, I learned that these artificial products were the repurposing of leftover deadly chemicals from World War II (Grewal 2022).

A Purposeful Life

These two early experiences contributed to my life's work of researching what works and what doesn't to create the balance and harmony in our bodies and in Nature. If we are serving our own health, it naturally flows to the planet and vice versa. They are inextricably linked. It has informed much of the work and studies I have pursued in my life.

As a young child around eight, an interesting incident happened that I forgot about for many years. The memory returned at a perfect time to remind me I am connected to something bigger than myself, a Higher Intelligence that holds a plan for me. I came here to live a purposeful life.

Something jogged my memory decades later, and the situation and feelings revisited me. I remembered feeling my back leaning against the swaying trunk of my special tree as I sat in my rudimentary treehouse. It was my retreat place, a place I could be free, observe, dream, and wonder about all sorts of things.

I remember tuning in to the sound of the whispering wind moving through the pine needles, mesmerised by its insistent hypnotic sound carrying the mystical messages of life. My little body surrendered to the gentle movement of the trunk in the breeze. I closed my eyes and felt myself go deep within, later to return to consciousness with an awareness of a message, something like: *One day people of this world will go through something very big and very bad, and I will be needed to play my part at that time.*

I wasn't the least bit perturbed by this message. Odd stuff was already part of my reality. I kept it to myself, and the memory buried itself deep until the day it resurfaced into conscious awareness decades later. My strong sense was that humanity would come through dark times and triumphs, and I would be here to bear witness to that. That time is now. It ramped up in early 2020. It may be the time for you to play your part too—we all have a unique piece of the jigsaw puzzle.

My mother confessed to me as a young adult years later that she often wondered where I came from. She knew I was different but never made it an issue, and I am grateful. I always knew I came from Creator. Then, I shelved that awareness as a young adult, as I allowed myself to be distracted and seduced by the sophistications and allure of modern life. I was on a steep learning curve trying to understand and integrate the ways of the world.

It's been a life-long journey that continues on.

Learning From Nature

What if our bodies and our environment speak to us all the time, and inspiration is all around us? We can learn so much if we remain open and curious. Trees, or Mother Nature generally, can offer us a safe space to be, support and protection, kindness, unconditional acceptance, steadfastness, and a different perspective if we attune ourselves. A tree helps us clear our minds, let go of worries, relax, breathe more deeply of the oxygen it provides for us. We feel better. Nature is an integral part of our survival.

Have you ever experienced anything like that? A moment when you felt that you would be needed sometime for something bigger, that your life held purpose? I suggest the time is now. Even if you don't know what it is or how it might come about.

Spend some time pondering that. Set an intention to remember what that purpose might be, even just a sense of it, or a wisp of a dream. Those senses are real; they came to you for a reason. Trust an answer will come.

When you embrace and work the principles and tools ahead, you will be clearer about who you are, why you have gathered certain unique life experiences and skillsets, what you can do with your gained wisdom to help others, and the first steps to take to make it happen.

Exercise

What are some of the early experiences you've had and the learnings you've gained with a little hindsight that contributed to shaping your life?

Spend time pondering that question and journal about it and see what unfolds for you.

I invite you to close your eyes, relax deeply in your body, slow your breath, and allow yourself to drift back to a time when you felt that perhaps a Higher Intelligence was communicating with you. Lean into the feelings of that experience. Breathe deeply and allow sensations to fill your whole body.

> - What vision comes to mind? Notice the feelings and name them if you can.
> - Track any colours, light and dark. What sounds or smells may have been present?
> - What was the message you received?
>
> If words don't come forward, try to capture your sense of it. Don't worry if a memory doesn't come to mind yet. It will. Simply make a clear intention and be open to different answers dropping in. Wonder what that answer might be. When it does land, tune in to the possibilities and insights that may float into your awareness.
>
> Capture them and journal.

Processing Grief

On the morning of my eleventh birthday, I awoke with a terrible sense of impending doom.

I did not want to be eleven.

I felt something bad was going to happen,

I had to grow up. I couldn't have fun anymore.

My world would be different.

I was inconsolable as my mother tried to calm my hysterical outburst.

Two months later, the phone rang in the wee hours of the morning, and I heard my mother emit a deep primal groan. She had just been told, by someone half a world away, that her only son, my brother, had died in a light plane accident in Alaska. I heard the voices, emotional and brittle, from my parents' bedroom.

I felt disturbed but must have eventually gone back to sleep and awoke to the news in the morning. Our household went silent and never fully recovered. We were all trapped in our grief. The sorrow was palpable. There was no conversation at all around grief: how to process it, how to honour it, how to find reconciliation within, how to integrate and be able to move forward.

All I remember is a quiet house filled with gladiolus flowers and the occasional sombre visitor. The loss for all of us was acute. I had three days away from school and then was sent back into *normal* life.

I was only able to process his loss as an adult. I had felt terribly guilty as I was the only member of the family who had not written anything to him, and he had asked me to.

What can an eleven-year-old contribute? I thought.

As an adult, I chose to write him a letter, telling him how much I missed him—his laughter, his loudness as he played the drums with the cutlery on the kitchen table, his sweetness, his mischief and sense of fun, and his interest in me as his littlest sister, always checking in with me to see how I was doing. I wrote what was in my Heart, kept it for a while, and when I felt ready, I burned the letter in a little ceremony of gratitude and respect.

I lived my life without the guiding hand of my brother and still miss him and others I have lost. But I remain grateful for the time we had together and the caring memories. Importantly, I now see my sensitivity, my ability to see and know things, as a great asset and gift.

Venturing Into the Wider World

I began my working life as a secretary. There were few choices available to women in the 1960s and early 70s in the country: secretary, nurse, teacher, hairdresser, shop assistant, all with a not so hidden expectation that we were filling in time until we got married and had children.

I worked in the private and public sectors, including a short stint as a secretary/jillaroo on a large cattle station in the centre of Australia. I loved the outback, the colours, the smells of the earth, and unique vegetation. I also loved going up in the Piper Cherokee with my boss to check that the bores were working. I freaked when he handed the controls over to me, and I felt the plane start to dip. He roared with laughter. He was also capable of roaring with anger if something didn't go his way.

I was acutely uncomfortable with the behaviour and patronising attitude of the dominant culture towards our original peoples, whose land has never been ceded under any treaty. It was painful for me to witness the dispossession of their dignity, culture, and custodianship of the land. I didn't even know the word *racism*. I was so embarrassed and felt such shame that some people could treat others so dismissively and disrespectfully, based on skin colour and cultural differences.

There was a moment that subtly changed my world. As part of my duties, I organised and distributed some basic supplies to the original peoples that lived and worked on the station. These consisted of *food* items, such as refined white flour and sugar, tinned apricot jam, tea plus aspirin, tobacco and stockman's clothing from R.M. Williams, a prestigious brand name in Australia.

The owner of the station wanted his workers to look good but fed them what I would consider nutritionless food. Their traditional food—flour from grasses, fruits from the earth, trees and bushes, and native animals like kangaroo, snake, and witchety grubs—had been vastly depleted by the cattle.

I handed a small pile to this particular gentleman. To me, he looked ancient. He could have been in his 30s and just lived a hard life. Our eyes locked for a moment. I saw such deep pain, and I felt it in my body. The next instant, I saw past the pain into the infinite constellations of mystery and possibility. I didn't understand feeling other people's feelings in my body at the time, and it shocked me. Having no language nor context to explain it to myself, I stuffed the memory down and buried it until it came up for me to process while writing this book.

I was a raw nineteen-year-old with little awareness of what was happening or why. My troubled emotions eventually resulted in sickness and a visit from the Royal Flying Doctor Service in remote Australia. I soon left for the next adventure, never forgetting my experiences or my feelings about what I had witnessed.

After several more years, I became secretary to the head of a government department and was so very excited about the possibilities for doing good in the world. A few years later, disgruntled feelings began to arise as I realised that people and the planet were not being prioritised.

One day, a document authored by my boss landed on my desk. It had not been typed by me. I read it and was mortified by its implications. I walked into his office and asked why he had not asked me to type it up.

He looked up at me, hesitated a second, and said, "Because I knew you wouldn't."

I was stunned. I told him he was right. While I was pleased that he knew I had ethics, I also experienced an uneasy feeling. I was very good at my job except for one thing. I had a conscience, and I was no longer a good fit for that job.

I figured that if I got a university degree, I would be able to make a bigger difference. I entered university as a *mature age student* at twenty-six. I had to sit for an aptitude test by writing an essay. I chose a topic on whether Aboriginal history should be included in the teaching of Australian history.

It seemed a ludicrous question to me. Of course, it should be included and truthfully told—which still hasn't happened to this day. I did not have enough science in my educational background to study for a science degree, but they did allow me to do two half-subjects of science. I chose Botany and Physics, Man, and Society—which was a physics subject for lay people—both of which I excelled at.

At the beginning of my studies in 1980, my oldest sister was diagnosed with cancer at age thirty-three. She had surgery to remove a slow-growing tumour—no chemo or radiation, just regular checkups—and is still with us today. At the end of that year, my father passed away from a second stroke at age sixty-four. Way too young. The year before, both my grandparents had also passed.

It was a time of great loss, grieving, learning, integrating. I had to learn that bad things happen that I may not understand but needed to accept as they were out of my control. I knew I had to keep my focus on what was good in my life, to grieve as healthily as I knew how, to love, to let go, and be grateful.

I forged ahead with my part-time studies, learning new things, covering new ground. I received my Bachelor of Arts degree in 1985 with a double major in Social Geography, which is the study of human populations and their needs, and Physical Geography, which covered biodiversity and explored the natural forces that shape landforms.

I went back into government to work in Native Vegetation Retention and Coastal Protection. It didn't take long for me to realise I would not be able to really contribute to the change I wanted to see, and a couple of years later, I left that job to more patient, capable, and resourceful people than myself at the time.

I have absolutely no regrets about my years of study. Knowledge is critical, and I still draw on it to this day.

More Tragedy

Two days before one of my university final year exams in 1984, my second eldest sister passed away, five months after diagnosis of cancer at thirty-three years of age—the same age as my oldest sister. I was stressed to the eyeballs, exhausted, and must have been on autopilot through Divine intervention to pass that exam.

During the test, I was vaguely aware of something strange going on in my body, specifically my face. I went to the bathroom afterwards, and as I was washing my hands, I looked up into the mirror and saw half my face had dropped. I had a half grimace. It was Bell's Palsy, a temporary paralysis of my face.

I was already at rock bottom, deeply distressed and miserable, and that was another blow to deal with. I also had to withdraw from an upcoming field trip I had been looking forward to all year—to the desert country as part of my studies. I couldn't risk getting any dust into my eyes as one now did not close properly. More salt to the wound.

My sister's death impacted me deeply as she had experienced years of pain and misdiagnosis. Because the doctors could not find a reason, she was told it was all in her head, as if she were imagining the pain. They eventually decided to do exploratory surgery, opened her up, and soon closed her up again as the cancer had spread throughout much of her body.

I remember being appalled at her treatment and intuitively knew something was deeply flawed in the system as I watched her in hospital, being fed white bread, ham-and-mustard sandwiches and weak, milky sugary tea. Zero nutrition. These were the days when medicine did not acknowledge lack of appropriate nutrition and chronic stress as contributors to disease in the body.

After she passed, I sat on the floor of my bedroom exhausted with grief, staring at the light playing on the moving curtain at the open window and silently asked, *If something good can come out of this, please show me.*

Educational Kinesiology

My next passion was calling me in the natural health arena. I couldn't afford the time nor money for another degree. Naturopathy would have been my choice at the time, but then I discovered *educational kinesiology*, which enabled me to work with children and adults with learning difficulties and minor health issues. I loved this work and the results it could bring to people using non-invasive techniques to reduce emotional stress, build new neural pathways, and retrain the brain to switch on to whole brain learning more effectively. The side benefits were improved health and happiness. It was exciting, cutting-edge work in the mid-1980s in the fields of learning and health, though it was not acknowledged in the mainstream. Through word-of-mouth, we had a never-ending supply of clients.

I like to think I was practicing neuroplasticity before it became a term! I learned so much about the intrinsic intelligence of the human body and its energy systems—called meridians—that feed our organs to deliver good health. I also learned about the emotions assigned to these organs and meridians, which contribute to imbalances in the body and can lead to disease unless resolved.

For example, resentment and anger are stored in the liver and its partner gall bladder. If we live in the state of anger or resentment for a long time, it will impact those organs. Grief and sadness reside in the lungs and large intestine areas. If we do not process those emotions to release the story that has created them, our lungs and large intestine can be affected.

This understanding was sourced in Traditional Chinese Medicine, which has been practised for thousands of years. There is a similar practice of acupuncture in India as old if not older.

I learned we are electrical beings first before we are biological beings. We are energy atoms before we are a cell. Electrical energy informs the physical body of imbalances in the energy channels. Pain is considered blocked energy in the meridians that are fed by the chakras—energy centres in the body—associated with particular organs and emotions.

If not resolved, these blockages can eventually express in the physical body. This can cause anything from joint pain and diabetes to heart problems or cancer. Pain is a symptom, a message from the body consciousness that change is needed. It will keep showing up, perhaps growing bigger and louder if we don't deal with the underlying story of whatever may have happened, and specifically, the meaning we made about ourselves.

This is valuable information to take on board, because we tend to blame the body. Our body serves us brilliantly until it can't anymore because of our choices, our actions, or inactions.

Spiritual Studies

During this time, I also serendipitously found a source of spiritual teachings that were so simple, practical, and profound they seamlessly fit into my life, stretched and expanded my consciousness in ways that humbled and challenged me, and evolved my thinking and understanding of myself and human potential. I became an ordained minister in the Church for Movement of Spiritual Inner Awareness (MSIA) in 1988.

In 2000, I graduated with a Master of Spiritual Science. This training was so impactful for me I repeated the coursework two more times over the next ten years, each time raising my level of experience and understanding of myself and life.

Without a doubt, these studies changed my life. I became a spiritual scientist, testing techniques on myself to see what worked, what served my health and happiness, and what allowed me to create a personal relationship with the Divine.

After a few years of practicing educational kinesiology, I left that work to pursue my next passion, raising my two children. Marriage and children turned my world on its head, with challenges and demands nobody could ever have prepared me for. Fortunately, the rewards were many as I witnessed two amazing little beings grow up and emerge into adulthood, albeit with their own set of challenges and adventures.

They are now well-adjusted, well-informed, kind, compassionate, conscious adults with their own children to shepherd in an ever-increasing complex and chaotic world. We are all blessed to have our inner compass pointing to the simple, sustainable, close-to-earth, natural way of life.

Bioresonance Therapy

After ten years spent full-time mothering, I heard about a new health practice called bioresonance therapy, which uses an energy machine with electromagnetic frequencies to detect substances, such as viruses, bacteria, allergies, and heavy metals in the body and to treat pathogens by inverting the energy signature of that pathogen. I had one session and wanted to learn more. I was in the first training in Australia in 2000.

It was a steep learning curve for me as it felt like I was hearing and reading a totally foreign language and couldn't make head nor tail of it. A couple of weeks before the exam, I reread all the modules and all my notes, and finally it all fell into place. Huge relief. I passed with flying colours.

I learned everything is energy, and everything has a frequency, its unique energy signature. We are electrical-magnetic beings ourselves in a biological suit called a body. There are signals conducive to the good health of our body, and there are other frequencies that interfere with our body's abilities to work efficiently.

When our own unique frequency is lowered due to chronic stress from physical, chemical, and radiation sources, plus emotional and mental issues, our immune system can become compromised, and we are more susceptible to illness.

After some years of doing bioresonance therapy, I started to see limitations as people were not always willing to take personal responsibility for their health and wanted something outside of themselves to fix them—such as going to a doctor to be given a pill or potion for whatever was ailing them without changing any of their habits that led to the imbalance or illness in the first place.

For many years, I had been researching natural health solutions that could be introduced into people's daily lives to improve their health and boost their chances of preventing disease. I had always been interested in natural remedies, the original medicine. I used these principles and practices to keep my frequency as high as possible.

Health and Wellbeing Coaching

I eventually moved into health and wellness coaching. I knew I had a lot of great information about health, but I soon realised I did not have the level of skill I wanted and needed to facilitate changing habits and self-identity. I needed some coaching and mindset skills. I found fabulous training at the Women-Centred Coaching Academy developed by the brilliant Dr. Claire Zammit and became trained in transformational coaching, facilitation, and leadership.

I loved it! The training was excellent, the community was amazing, and the change was profound. I love to work with women to assist them to own their innate worthiness, encouraging them to see their gifts and talents and to co-create a plan to manifest the life that is calling them forward.

CHAPTER 5

My Turning Points for Change

The year 2010 was a year of convergence for our family. My son left home, my daughter finished university, my husband retired, and I was completing the coursework of my master's degree for a third time. In my final sharing of my project and the experience and insights I had gathered—feeling incredibly grateful and proud for all I had achieved—an interesting energy presented itself, a feeling somewhere between unsettled nervousness and mild dread. I had a strong sense something big was on its way that I could no longer avoid.

Doing the spiritual work had alerted me to serious incongruences in my life, especially in my marriage. The vast mismatch between who I was at my core, my true nature, and how I was showing up in the marriage and our family situation was something I was no longer willing to tolerate. Utilising certain tools, I had begun to excavate my true nature, my True Self who was hidden behind the self-recriminations and labels I had accumulated. I was dismantling the façade of an old structure, brick by brick. Change was well and truly on its way.

Adolescent Son

When my son was going through his adolescence and teenage years, it was a difficult time for all of us. He was frustrated and angry at school, the system, parents, life in general. Suddenly around fourteen, he seemed to turn from a sweet, funny, wise, tuned-in little boy into an alien—someone I barely recognised—with a ton of anger, and most of it seemed to be directed towards me. His behaviours were disrespectful, uncooperative, and hurtful.

I kept questioning and undermining myself, asking what I had done wrong. *I must be a really bad mother to have such an unhappy child.* Where had I failed? Why couldn't I fix the situation or make him happier and nicer?

The meaning I took from this was that I was a failure. My self-identity had become wrapped up in my roles as mother and wife. All the evidence in front of me said I was clearly not doing very well on either front. As long as I didn't challenge him or his behaviours, the situation was barely tolerable.

He was a young man emerging into the world, and I felt he needed wisdom and support from his dad. However, his father was not available as he was struggling with his own issues keeping a business afloat. I was beginning to suffer from anxiety, withdrawing from interactions with others, desperately unhappy and losing confidence.

I believed if I kept showing up, being nice, and caring and doing as much as possible to keep the peace, the situation would eventually change. Right? Wrong. Insanity.

Have you heard the saying that doing the same thing over and over again and expecting a different result is insanity?

I qualified.

Learning to Love It All

I was grasping for meaning, some understanding of what was going on and how I could change it. I remembered one of the teachings my spiritual teacher taught me: *You need to learn to love it all.*

He said this was a simple concept but not always an easy thing to do. His words irritated me, circling in the background while I continually avoided them. I always railed against that fundamental teaching.

How could I love this?

How could I love the behaviour of someone venting their anger towards me daily?

How could I love the behaviour that made me feel like a doormat and worthless?

I was doing my absolute best to stay loving, but I could not love the situation nor the behaviours.

One day, sitting in the sun mulling over things, I asked Spirit if there was another way of looking at this situation, so I could make a different meaning. I knew I couldn't keep going on in the same way. Awareness dropped in. I had tried everything, except one thing—loving it all.

I felt the energy shift as I pondered this. I changed angles in my vision and began to wonder how I could love this situation. I started with sarcasm: *I really love when this happens. I really love when he explodes at me. I really love having lots of opportunity to explore disrespect and dysfunctionality.* I went into an entire rant that eventually changed from sarcasm to ridiculousness, which changed the whole energy. I ended up laughing at the sheer absurdity of a situation that was so unlovable and felt so destructive to me, my self-worth, my son's sense of self, and our relationship.

I knew I loved my son beyond his behaviours; that was unshakeable. I knew who he was beneath them. I never learned to love the behaviours, but I accepted them and the situation as a learning opportunity. I learned to see my value and worth differently. I could love myself unconditionally because of my innate goodness and loving nature, regardless of anyone else's opinion.

I was not a perfect mum by any means, but I was able to love unconditionally beyond the behaviours. Critically, I could see that I was truly good at something. That realisation was a turning point. My self-esteem began to rise.

Things improved. He eventually grew up and left home. Then he returned several months later, and things grew decidedly worse again. I was being presented with another opportunity to get it right, because I obviously needed more practice at maintaining my internal space.

After a few months, I chose to give him a choice: Either be more pleasant and helpful or find another place to live. The effect was immediate. He packed a bag and left. Relief flooded my body. I knew he had good friends and could make good decisions. I trusted he would be safe. He was.

After a couple of weeks, I started sending texts to say I hoped he was happier and that I loved him. I never asked any questions because I knew he would baulk at that. He was an adult and could make choices and wear the consequences of those. Painfully, I recognised it was none of my business. I had to let go and allow myself and him to grow.

A few months later, we met and reconciled. It was awkward, but it was a start for a new adult relationship which has blossomed over the years.

Not Taking Things Personally

When I stopped making the situation all about me—what a bad mother I must be—there was an opportunity to see circumstances differently. Eventually, I understood that his Soul was reaching out to me, rather insistently, to get him out of the situation. He had done his learning with us and needed a different environment in which to grow and learn.

I knew I had put in as much good, loving-kindness as I could in those critical early years. I could sense the beautiful caring, loving, kind man he would become.

I learned that a different meaning can always be made, that meanings can be about the other person's sense of self, not my self-worth. There is such a great need for training in emotional intelligence and how to develop and utilise it in all relationships—starting with our relationship with ourselves.

Breakdown to Breakthrough

At the same time, I was dealing with my husband's stress of running a business during difficult economic times. He spent long hours at work and came home drained and exhausted. We argued often over money, compounded by the fact that I was not earning and, therefore, was dependent on him. His preferred methods of stress relief were wine and my body. He was not an alcoholic—never got drunk— and was not physically abusive. He simply was of the mindset that still pervades many cultures: he believed his wife's body was his property for his use.

"A man has rights," he said to me. In my chronic confusion, my dire lack of self-esteem, and inability to connect with any resourcefulness to make sense of the comment and produce a reasonable comeback, I agreed with him. It didn't even occur to me that I had rights, too, especially over my own body.

My behaviour truly reflected my deep disconnection from myself and my feelings. I had constantly overridden my feelings because I wasn't prepared to see that my life was not happy. My feelings didn't fit my story of a happy family and life, and I so desperately wanted that story after my childhood loss of my brother and the sadness that ensued.

I was drowning in the shame from the stories I was telling myself of not being a good wife, not meeting his needs. I was inadequate, deficient, unworthy, and a burden. I felt like I had no choice but to submit to keep the peace in order to avoid the cold silence. I wanted and needed his approval because I was sure as heck not giving that to myself.

I had to override and disconnect from my feelings of hurt from not being seen, not feeling valued, and his unwillingness to hear me when I tried to discuss it with him. He did not seem to have the capacity to understand, and I clearly didn't have the capacity to articulate it in a way that he could understand. I was a mess and felt betrayed, misunderstood, diminished, and objectified.

This was not what I signed up for, I thought. My confidence plummeted. I was losing myself; I didn't know who I was anymore.

Somehow, I hid the truth of my deep unhappiness from everyone, including myself. My visible story was life was good. I had a loving, attentive husband, great kids, and wonderful friends. I could not understand why I was so miserable. I was living a double life and didn't recognise it. I kept these two stories separate, a result of the vast disconnect from myself, my emotions, and my Truth.

On the Edge

By 2012, I knew I was in real trouble. My sanity had reached the tipping point of tumbling into oblivion. In January, my son left home. It lightened the load for a time, but it didn't change the story. I was at a breaking point. I knew with every fibre of my being that if I did not physically remove myself from home, I would die. It was that matter of fact. I was barely functional.

I had suggested a couple of times that I needed a break, and my husband agreed. He encouraged me to go away for a few weeks to sort myself out and then come home. He said he would be waiting for me. To him, I obviously needed to sort myself out and would return home soon, sorted. Women were complex and overemotional, and somehow, that was a weakness. I was co-author to that story.

Leaving Home

I made arrangements with a friend who had a little cottage to rent in a small town by the ocean. The previous lease had just finished, creating a perfect time for me to move in for a little while. It was such a blessing to have somewhere to go.

Before leaving, I spent a week or two sorting out what I needed, then did all the washing, cleaning, and cooking to make things easier for everyone. I fed the story of *good little wife and caring mother*, showing my husband how to cook a few meals and teaching him how to use the washing machine.

I packed my little car to the gunnels and off I sailed into the wild blue yonder. I had no idea what was ahead of me, none. If I had thought too deeply about it—the consequences or repercussions—I would have panicked. So, I put off pondering and put off panicking and put my foot to the accelerator. It was a clear blue sky with one little heart-shaped cloud. I took it as a good omen.

For a few weeks, I felt like I was in a protective bubble. I was calm, almost happy as a result of removing myself from a stressful destructive situation. I didn't even allow guilt to visit much.

Weeks turned into months, and reality set in. I was on my own. It was winter. Days were short; nights were long. The terrors started visiting me. I moaned and groaned and wailed in the middle of the night, wanting to hide and be swallowed up. I became nervy and restless. I couldn't sleep. A rash broke out on my face and hands. I felt bereft, lonely, and lost.

My only companion most days was the ocean, which, in winter, was very dramatic. I walked the beach for hours and came back with numb feet from the cold sand and water. I felt free with the ocean. I loved its constancy and its ever-changing nature and always felt refreshed and renewed. Until I got home, and the stories would spring up and haunt me again.

I texted my daughter often and spoke to my husband regularly, which was always challenging. Every two to three weeks, I visited home for a night or two. As soon as I walked in the front door, I felt my legs go weak, but the need to work this situation out was greater than my fear of coming back.

These visits were brittlely awkward times, eggshell territory. Communication was difficult, fraught with misunderstandings and recriminations. But I persisted. As confused as I still was, I was clear about one thing—this was not just about me. This was about both of us.

Remembering My Tools

After a few more weeks, I remembered I had tools for clearing negativity, and a little ray of hope and sunshine entered my space. How could I have forgotten?

I was overwrought for so long, old stories on a repeat loop ad infinitum: *He did such and such, said this or that, treated me badly. I've been wronged.* The loop played and on and on so there was little room for a new awareness or new narrative to come in. Now that I had the space to remember, I set about using these tools.

I was on a mission of saving myself, of understanding what the heck happened to two good people in what seemed like a good marriage. I was so traumatised by the situation and the stories I was telling myself about my perceived inadequacies, I knew I needed to be gentle with myself. I wanted to go all the way to healing this situation. I couldn't see any future for us without addressing it.

I calmed myself down with deep breathing and meditation, visualising things I loved, things I was grateful for. I placed my hand on my Heart and created safety within myself for that traumatised part of me to be seen and heard. I directed my attention inwards and turned towards that part instead of away, which had been my previous pattern.

I previously had not wanted to move too close to the pain in case I couldn't handle it, allowing it to swamp me. I brought the loving-kindness and compassion that I easily shared with others and entered into the relational field with this traumatised aspect of myself, this part I had been avoiding for years. She was trapped in a story and isolated because her trauma was not being addressed.

The pattern was triggered, repeating itself ad infinitum, waiting until I could process the emotions associated with the story I was telling myself, the story based on my perceptions and interpretations of what was happening. The perpetuation of the story and my hurt emotions kept the trauma going until I could no longer handle the retelling of the story and the meaning I was making of it.

I felt a yawning chasm away from healing, but I was determined, diligent and applied the tools. Eventually, the resistance began to dissolve. I cleared enough to gain some clarity about the stories. I gained altitude to rise above the pain and see the stories more objectively, creating distance from the story and its associated emotions.

This distance helped me change my attitude to one of curiosity and inquiry into the situation. I put on my spiritual scientist hat and got working.

Acceptance

The first step was acceptance, even if I couldn't understand what was going on or in no way condoned what had happened. Reality was present, in my face, and I needed to accept that. The story I had told myself of perpetrator and victim, predator and prey, dominance and submission seemed so real and true to me. My nervous system could attest to that.

Taking Personal Responsibility

I knew I had to go deep to see where my personal responsibility lay.

I asked these questions:

- What had I allowed, promoted, and co-created with my husband?
- How had I been showing up that enabled those behaviours to continue?
- Where was I abandoning myself?

That last question did it. I cried and cried like a baby, or like a woman brought starkly face-to-face with her actions and inactions, and her unaware, well-meaning, self-destructive beliefs and behaviours. Understanding that I had abandoned myself over and over, year in-year out, was almost more than I could bear.

My life was overlaid with so many skewed stories of powerlessness, non-possibilities, duty, wifely responsibilities, doing the right thing, and being nice—all at the cost of my sense of self, my sanity, my self-esteem, my worthiness, and my ability to respond in healthy constructive ways. It seemed like I had turned into a 1950s housewife, when men made all the decisions and women cooperated. I was so overwhelmed with feelings of shame, guilt, regret, and desperation, I felt myself drifting into oblivion.

Allowing Breakdown

It was at that moment of realising what I had co-created that I was brought undone, and my reality collapsed. My knees buckled and I fell to the floor. It was scary. There were no reference points anymore; nothing made sense. I felt like I couldn't fall any further; I had reached that *bottom of the barrel* moment.

Except—I couldn't feel the bottom. I was descending into nothingness. I was like a mud puddle, formless, detached from any reality. I had no access to my physical body, my rational mind, or any feeling. I was numb, floating in strange waters, unable to get my bearings, any sense of where I was or how to navigate out of there. I was in a state of shock and numbness, unable to relate to the situation or myself. I have no idea how long I laid there in quasi-land.

Sometime later, after wallowing in the murky waters, I became aware of dappled light and shadow from the late afternoon sun playing on the walls. The energy was shifting; there now seemed to be a possibility of a lifeline within reach. I could feel this new energy moving through my body, reweaving my shattered nervous system and reshaping reality.

I now realise that I probably experienced a nervous breakdown.

Being brought undone by my realisations led to feeling powerless, crushed, even stupid, because I could see how I contributed to perpetuating the situation. This was actually the moment when everything began to change. I was able to see my part, my Truth, and allowed everything else to fall away. Nothing else could exist when I came face-to-face with my Truth and owned it.

When I went to the depths of vulnerability, all the illusions, old stories, and whatever props I had for keeping them in place vanished. Therefore, I felt adrift. I was removed from my old stories. Who was I without these stories informing me? This place felt different, unknown and scary. My old reality had been running on my old stories and associated feelings and repeating themselves ad infinitum, filling the whole space with less-ness, wrongness, and confusion.

I now had a pathway out. I had the power to change the situation by taking responsibility, owning my part in the co-creation of the situation and the resulting meaning I made of it about myself and others that created the story and perpetuated the experience. I was starting to see and sense a whole new possibility for myself. I was gaining clarity about who I was and who I was not—and what I was no longer willing to tolerate—and that knowledge allowed me to begin to create a new story of power and possibility.

I knew that situation would never occur again because I was different. My energy was different. My old story had collapsed. My belief was different. My frequency was higher because I now had greater awareness and clarity.

I sat with all of this for several days and then went home with my newfound awareness. Driving down the driveway, I felt the panic rising in me again. My husband saw I was on a knife's edge and kindly asked what I needed.

I asked him to sit down and listen, and to please refrain from saying a word. I needed to talk until I was done. I told him there was no need to comment after I had finished unless he wanted to.

Truth-telling

I took a deep breath and allowed the wisdom of my Heart to voice my Truth, to be heard and witnessed. I was quite emotional and blubbered my way through—what I had allowed, what I had participated in, how it made me feel, and what I would no longer tolerate.

Voicing my Truth changed everything. When I took responsibility for my part, I was no longer a victim. I was a creator and, therefore, could now create something else. When I spoke my truth, when I named what I had co-created, I physically felt the bonds break apart in my body, the manacles unshackle. It was as if a spell had been broken. I interrupted the pattern by bringing it out of my unconscious into consciousness, naming it, feeling the feelings, and witnessing my pain.

I knew I would never co-create that story again. I would never abandon myself again. I felt freedom flood into my body; the energy of my power as my True Self returned. I aligned with my Truth of being a sovereign being, worthy purely because I exist, being lovable simply for who I am. I was now powerful to effect change in my life. The constrictions and limitations burst wide open, and expansion and Light flooded in.

This was my moment of breakdown to breakthrough, my emergence from the dark night of the Soul. I was creating a new story of me, my life, my world. I created a different experience, a new reality for myself and my relationships.

I didn't need my husband to change; I didn't need any validations. I was done and believed my marriage was over. I was free. I felt like I had punched through the illusion of disempowerment and fear to a new reality of possibility in my life, of loving-kindness to myself, of being my own best friend. I could now show up more fully as me, my True Self—my unique, quirky, curious, funny, loveable, courageous, powerful self—and begin to create a new self-identity, a new reality, a new life.

Releasing Old Story

My old story was of being a victim, not having a voice, and believing I didn't matter. I existed to make others happy, and if they weren't happy, it must be my fault. The meaning I made was I was a failure. In a world where I believed I was a victim, was responsible for everyone's happiness, and others were out to get me, what hope did I have of leading a balanced, happy life?

It's a common story, and we all have our own version of feeling victimised. Believing we are a victim makes us powerless, as we believe we can't change the situation. Taking responsibility for what your part is in the story is the first step to accessing your power to change it.

We can often devalue, diminish, and make ourselves wrong based on other people's opinions. It bites at our core identity. When we make other people's opinions irrelevant and none of our business, there is an opening for our self-identity to shift. We are more in charge. We become the architects of our own life, and we can change the trajectory of our life towards what we truly want, instead of what feels like settling for our fate, our lot in life.

Have you ever noticed yourself saying words to yourself, such as: *You're worthless, stupid, not enough or too much, or you're wrong or bad*? Negative self-talk can be incredibly damaging. If you don't value yourself—usually based on a belief that someone else may have started—you lower your own frequency and broadcast that into the collective field, and someone of a similar frequency will show up in your space to prove you right. This does not mean that other people don't have a responsibility in hurting you. It does mean that you have a responsibility to communicate kindly to and support yourself.

An energetic field flows through and around all of us—and indeed all of existence—that creates our reality through our experiences. My low frequency of unworthiness that I was broadcasting to the field was attracting others to prove me right. They had no idea they were participating in my story of unworthiness. Neither did I.

Reclaiming Sovereignty

It was one of the most pivotal moments of my life—reclaiming my sovereignty, my power. That power was always present within me to make a different choice, but it seemed I had to reach a desperation point of feeling like I was dying—to feel like I had lost everything, including my sanity—to be able to access it and take a different approach.

I learned that by coming into acceptance of the situation, opening to new awareness, suspending my judgements, my old stories, and erroneous beliefs, everything began to shift. When I took responsibility for my part in what I co-created, enabled, and allowed and sought a different awareness and perspective, I acknowledged that I was a creator: a very powerful concept.

I was no longer a victim. If I didn't like what I had contributed to, mostly unconsciously, I could begin to consciously co-create something new and different that served me, my health, and my peace of mind.

Creating a New Story

You have a responsibility to think well of yourself, regardless of anyone else's opinion, to line up with Truth that you are worthy purely because you exist. You are part of Creation just like everyone else, even the bullies. Consider that maybe they are here to nudge you towards finding yourself beyond all the labelling and the false identities. They have their own stories going on.

Your job is to recognise and name all the goodness that you are, your willingness to contribute goodness to the world, and to own all the good things you do for others that uplifts them. Remind yourself daily. Be grateful for *you*. Your frequency will lift. Your experience will begin to change and, therefore, your reality.

If this sounds too simple, that's because it is simple. It's a matter of shifting your focus and telling a new story, even if it feels like you're making it up. You made up the meaning about yourself in the old story based on how you perceived and interpreted what happened to you in the past. Now you are creating a new story of power and possibility and lifting your vibration to be a match for what it is you desire to create in your life.

It may seem like the old imposter syndrome is rearing its head, but I invite you to consider that the real imposter syndrome is actually pretending to be anything less than the magnificence of who you really are by diminishing and devaluing yourself to make others more comfortable.

No more!

When I first spoke my Truth to myself and fully proclaimed it, it set me free and empowered me to begin to consciously co-create with the Universe a new story: healthy, self-supporting, and life-affirming. I utilised the Tools of Consciousness in Chapter 7. I made one conscious choice after another, starting with a new story of worthiness, inspired by the training I did with Dr Clair Zammit: *My pure existence is enough to be considered worthy.*

Vulnerability Is Powerful and Scary

I understand now that vulnerability and its depths, which feel so incredibly murky and terrorising, are actually the place from which growth is possible. There is nowhere else to go but inward.

What if the depths to which we descend are inversely proportional to the heights we can soar? What if allowing ourselves to feel our vulnerability is a gift of strength and courage and has enormous transformative potential to create meaningful change?

It may not feel like it, but when we come through those vulnerable times, we become warriors capable of changing our own lives and others' lives as well.

What if that place of numbness or terror or nothingness is just our old stories and beliefs falling away so we may feel adrift or empty?

We can then meet ourselves as raw, real, and ready for a different interpretation, a different story to invite ourselves into our true expression. Then, we are able to see who we are not, so that we can begin to recalibrate and reconfigure our lives to reveal who we truly are.

We Are Powerful Creators

It is also important to note that we don't need to implode or break down to see things differently, to make a different choice. Once I learned that my feelings were a powerful feedback system—when I acknowledged them, felt into them, named them, and recognised my need for self-acceptance, self-respect, and self-love—the situation calmed down because those aspects of my experience had been acknowledged and honoured. They reflected an aspect of me that was calling for understanding and resolution. I could now make a different choice in how I responded.

Recognising that I was a powerful creator and could create negatively or positively was a choice and a game changer. I learned to put myself first, prioritise my own wellbeing, review my sense of self in any situation, stand in my own self-worth, and not wait or seek anyone else's approval.

Exercise

To interrupt thoughts you don't want, ask yourself regularly:

Am I contributing to goodness in my life and the world— or not?

Journal about any clarity you gain over time.

The joy of knowing I could change my reality was life-changing, and I continued my journey into greater enlightenment with greater awareness and higher consciousness. It is always changing and evolving.

You are a powerful creator. You can choose to become a conscious creator of good things in your world that support yourself and can serve others. You can consciously choose what you are contributing to—being part of the solution and not the problem by remaining a victim.

Destiny versus Fate

You are either the master of your own destiny, or you keep doing and thinking the same old ways and settle for your fate. You can make choices based on aligning with who you are becoming, not who you have been. Your past has shaped you, but don't allow it to define you.

When you choose wisely and lovingly, you are adding to the Light in the world, lifting the frequency, transmuting the darkness, increasing goodness, and ameliorating some of the pain and suffering. You can be the sparkle that lights up others' lives.

As you transform and transmute your own story of pain, you become a bright Light, a beacon of hope for others. As we heal, we literally transmute the darkness from our shadows and transmit that Light out into the world.

Global Perspective

What if the story that was playing out within me and in my relationships can be compared to what is playing out in the world? What if the outer story of power play between the *haves* and *have nots*, controllers and controlled, perpetrators and victims, and the resulting helplessness, hopelessness, powerlessness of my inner story are reflecting each other? The microcosm and the macrocosm. As above, so below. As within, so outside. This is a powerful realisation. What if my inner world stories were being projected into the outer world? What if everyone's stories are being broadcast into the world?

Oh, what a change we can make when we heal our stories and transform our lives and that energy is then broadcast into the field.

It also speaks to the widespread betrayal of the patriarchal system from our governments, people in positions of power and authority in our institutions and corporations, who have abused their positions and inflicted abuse on the rest of the people. This is the toxic power-over, authoritarian, wounded Masculine model of power. Men are not inherently bad; neither are women weak. Both are strong, powerful, and caring and have different expressions of those traits. We have had some poor role models from people of influence, including many celebrities, that have become normalised into the culture.

Mutual Healing

Do I think my husband was a bad man? No, he was operating from the wounded Masculine within. He was a product of his upbringing and culture. He was, in fact, a good, kind man in so many ways, which is why I was so confused for so long. He just had dysfunctional ideas about women and marriage and projected those into our relationship.

I was also a product of that culture and had some unconscious, distorted ideas of what being a woman was—particularly in my wife and mother roles—until I went through the cathartic metamorphosis of breakdown to breakthrough. I drew a line in the sand, was clear about what I would no longer support, and healed the stories within myself.

Eventually, my husband did the inner work and began to heal some of his own stories. I still had more work to do to heal my anger, resentment, and grief over the loss of what seemed a good marriage. We did the work for ourselves, not each other. If we were ever going to be able to heal the marriage, we had to do it for ourselves first.

I also needed to restore trust and safety in myself first, to trust my own feelings and deeper knowing. Over time, we were able to rebuild trust and safety in the relationship, reconnect, and become good friends again. Fortunately love never died for either of us; however, our connection and trust took a battering. I could have easily left if we did not take responsibility for what we co-created together and did the inner work for ourselves. Otherwise, we had no chance of reconciliation.

My son and husband were two of my greatest teachers. They reflected back to me my dysfunctional beliefs about myself, my worth, my value. It was not good. But in all the sandpapering that happens in relationships, sometimes we are lucky to produce a polished gem.

Can I be grateful for it all? Yes, I can now. Especially that I did the work and freed myself from painful erroneous beliefs.

I was very clear about boundaries, and because he was willing to honour them, we stayed together. We have become kind, loving, considerate, fun partners for each other, which is how we started our relationship years ago. We had to come home to ourselves and remember our true natures to be the best version of ourselves to become best partners again.

Our Sacred Work

The task ahead of us is to witness our own stories and those of others, to acknowledge them as real and true, to reflect upon the pain of going through tough times, and to bring our loving compassion to ourselves and others so we can do the sacred work of healing. We are worth it. It is the only way forward—going within to create a better life and better world.

In the world, we are presently witnessing gross violations of freedom, dignity, and sovereignty being carried out, and inequities are being highlighted. It seems there are battles and pain inflicted everywhere.

There are many warmongers in positions of power. They peddle fear through the mainstream media to justify their actions and manipulate our perceptions through fashioning a particular narrative to target our emotions, so we respond in predictable ways. If people are fearful enough, they will even condone the actions of these warmongers.

There will never be world peace until there is inner peace in enough of us to lift the frequency of the world. In our love for ourselves and humanity, we can stand up and say, *Enough! No more!* and draw a line in the sand. We can push back nonviolently and speak our Truth.

Your voice matters; our voice matters. Maharishi Mahesh Yogi suggested that we only need 1 percent of the population to consciously raise their frequency to bring about change. The higher frequency will entrain the lower frequency, and we can all lift each other up (Roth 2012).

You might still be asking: *When will this situation end? Why me?*

The answers could differ from what you may have thought in earlier times. Whether it is personal or global, the situation ends when you say so, when you make a different choice on how you are seeing it and take different actions that lead to liberation from the story and the emotions that fuel it. It ends when you remember who you are. Practice the tools in Chapter 7 to support your new choices and actions.

Why you? Because you asked to go to the next level, and you asked for someone or something to enable you to raise you above and beyond where you have been. It never feels like it or looks like it at the time, but in hindsight, we can often see if *that* didn't happen, we could not have seen what was going on and how out of alignment we were with who we really are and what we really wanted. We are then able to make different choices and head in a different direction.

If our internal world of turmoil, struggle, and limitations is being reflected in the outer world, the way through would be to heal our internal reality—to resolve the stories, labels, judgements, guilt, fear, and doubts that we have on repeat loop. As we dissolve the negativity within ourselves, we add to the dissolution of that in the world.

Different tools are needed to view these stories of what has happened to us so that we may lovingly and compassionately come into relationship with them, to acknowledge, witness, and honour them, and reweave a new story of possibility for ourselves and our world.

To know yourself > is to love yourself > is to heal yourself > is to heal our world.

Imagine that when our thoughts are filled with lack and fear, they are like a little cloud above our heads, similar to cartoon captions. What if many others have the same thing going on? What if all the individual clouds reflecting our individual consciousnesses join up and feed into one big cloud that we could call *collective consciousness*? What if we healed ourselves and fed new, empowered stories into the collective field of consciousness?

Exercise

Consider we are not only feeding into but also sourcing from a controlling matrix of reality based on collective beliefs. How do we begin to unplug from this matrix and create a new reality?

Take the time to ponder these questions and journal about possible answers:

- What else is possible here?
- Is there another way of looking at it?
- What do I need to know, that if I did know, would change everything?
- What other options could I consider?

Making a different choice leads to a different result. It's a different equation.

Return of the Divine Feminine

I came back to live in the family home December 20, 2012, the day before the summer solstice in the southern hemisphere. I like to honour these special natural cycles, which in ancient times were celebrated as significant markers for change, signalling a time for inner work at the winter solstice and outer work at summer solstice.

The end of the Mayan calendar was much hyped. It did signify the ending of one cycle and beginning of a new. My daughter and I attended a ceremony to celebrate this auspicious occasion with input from local Indigenous musicians and artists. It was a lovely simple evening with beautiful people, and we came home pleased, yet mildly disappointed that nothing seemed to have happened to signify change. What were we expecting? Lights in the sky, clapping of thunder, and dramatic lightning?

Sometime later, I leaned into the energy of that solstice evening again. There was a subtle, new-yet-ancient energy coming to life. I was given a vision of a deserted, dried-up old spring in a remote place. Next, I saw the ground moisten, and the spring came to life and began to bubble as gentle spurts of water were ejected and began to tumble down the slope.

The water seemed gentle yet intentional, determined, and mission oriented. I understood the spring symbolised the return of the Divine Feminine that had been silenced and driven underground by what I would call the manipulation of the lower realms of light, the practice of black magic, terror, distortions, hypnosis, and mind control. She was returning to balance the power and will of the Masculine with the love and wisdom of the Feminine.

2020—Game On

I awakened early on the January 1, 2020, into what felt to be a very different energy. Forever curious, I leaned in to see what that might mean for me and our world. The words *Game on!* flashed into my brain, and I saw two fists coming together head on for impact, and I felt in my body the machinations engage for the age-old battle between good and evil, the forces of Light and the forces of Darkness in the biggest most visible way yet. The scale of it took my breath away. I didn't know what that meant at the time. This was the year the world changed irreversibly. We all know what happened in 2020.

As soon as I started hearing in the media what I recognised to be repetitive messaging, preparing us for something big from politicians, government agencies, and medical *experts* all around the world, I knew they were sowing the seeds for impending disaster. When I heard, "Experts fear this could be the worst catastrophe for humanity," I knew this was it. It was *Game on!* for the minds and bodies of humanity. We were being told how many cases were testing positive, heightening the fear, but rarely how many people had been hospitalised or had died.

I had treated coronavirus as a bioresonance therapist. I knew it to be a nasty flu that could take up to a week with lots of rest to recover for most otherwise healthy people. What was different about this strain? I was confused about why so many healthy people, not showing symptoms, were testing positive. Not showing symptoms used to mean our immune system was working well. Why was the government not giving advice to people on how to strengthen their immune system?

It is not the scope of this book to go into more details, but many respected doctors, scientists, lawyers, and researchers around the world have been delving deeply into this. A lot of answers have been revealed since, backed by copious amounts of evidence. If you would like to find out more, please check the Resources list in the back of this book.

A Different Lens

During this time, I became aware that I could switch between what I call the 3-D consciousness of our world of drama, control, and perspective management and a higher 5-D consciousness of love and peace that comes from beyond this reality. I had to rise from the drama and crises of this world to protect myself as media went into hyperdrive to whip up a frenzy of fear. Tech giants went into damage control to shut down any dissenting voices, including many well-respected doctors and scientists.

I found I could also witness the manoeuvrings, the rigging of narratives to elicit certain reactions and the lockstep response around the world. I had been able to shift my state to some degree for a while, but not to the extent of ease and clarity I now had. It was like I found a different portal or lens to look through that gave me multi-perspectives.

I could shift into the peace and calm and loving energy of the higher frequencies to be reassured events were all part of the Divine Plan, even though it didn't look like it or feel like it at all. It still doesn't look like Divine circumstances, but the energy is different now. So many more people have awakened and are on board.

I know humanity will win this primal battle of good and evil. I have known since I was eight years old, sitting in my tree. I knew it wasn't going to be easy, and everyone who felt called to do their part would have to stand up and speak their Truth.

That time is now.

CHAPTER 6

Know Thyself

The prime directive for humanity at this time is to know itself. That means starting with you knowing yourself at the deepest levels. It is critical. There is no bypass option if you want to make the difference you feel you are here to experience and bring to others. The task is massive, and if you choose to do this, the whole trajectory of your life will change. The entire Universe will conspire with you to bring this about.

My spiritual teacher would refer to the statue of David and say that David was already in the block of marble that Michelangelo sculptured. He just chipped away everything that was not David to reveal the beauty and majesty that was uniquely David.

It is the same with you, but you'll be using different tools. No chisels needed.

As you come into willingness to release everything that is not you, as you uncover the beliefs, labels, and endless stories of not being good enough and heal them with your loving compassion, you will begin to uncover the true you, your True Self. Once you utilise the Tools of Consciousness, you will notice those little changes; you will feel different, more connected, calmer, and happier. Little changes will lead to bigger changes, and soon you will be living a different life, one more aligned with your values.

If you could truly believe that you were born to make a difference, how perfect you might see your life to be! All of the life experiences you have gone through—all the challenges, the heartaches, the losses, the tough situations and feelings you endured, and all of the learnings you gained from them— have brought you to where you are now, poised and ready to learn new skills.

Are you ready to do the following:

- Release the need to do things the same way?
- Adopt a growth mindset?
- Develop and trust your intuition?
- Become comfortable with uncertainty?
- Utilise your innate and accumulated wisdom?
- Explore new possibilities?

As you experience more and more of your True Self, you will know what resonates for you and what aligns with your true values. Be willing to trust in the Universe/Higher Intelligence/ the Divine and let go of needing certainty in your life.

These are big asks maybe, but necessary to move forward into this new Earth we are co-creating. What if the Universe has your back and is conspiring on your behalf to reveal and manifest what you are here to do as you awaken to it?

Surrender the old ways of being in order to embrace the new, to change habits and ideas, to trust the process unique to you, to let go of any attachment to a particular outcome, and to be willing to act when needed. One step at a time.

Guidelines to Live Your Life By

Three powerful guidelines to living daily life were introduced to me by my spiritual teacher, John-Roger. They are simple and straightforward and require loving discipline as part of being a conscious, responsible co-creator as you learn to be loving and kind to yourself along this journey and course-correct where needed. They apply to all levels of being—physical, emotional, and mental—that contribute to you spiritually and expand your awareness.

Care for Yourself First

Take care of yourself first so you can help take care of others. We have been conditioned to think of this notion as selfish when it is actually self-supporting. If we don't take care of ourselves first, we not only compromise our ability to perform effectively in our own life, but also to offer a helping hand to others.

Do what you need to do to keep your life on an even keel and running well as much as possible. Then, you give from a full cup rather than a half-empty cup. It is like putting on your own oxygen mask first on flights, then helping others. If you have young children, I know priorities change, and it is challenging. Just do your best. That's all you can ask of yourself. It is a good lesson to share with children to respect *me-time*, their own and others.

Don't Hurt Yourself or Others

We can often hurt ourselves with unkind thoughts and words directed to ourselves. We would not say to our friends or a child some things we say to ourselves. Start treating yourself as your own best friend and learn to laugh with yourself. Practise being kind to yourself, and your health, happiness, and self-esteem will soar. Extend the same to others and watch relationships bloom.

This also includes our habits and behaviours that can hurt us physically. If you have these habits, it may be time to re-assess what works and what doesn't to support your health and wellbeing.

Are you self-supporting or self-sabotaging? Are you numbing or enlivening? Remember to be kind as you uncover the reality for yourself.

Use It All

Use everything for your learning, growth, advancement, and eventual upliftment.

I invite you for just a moment to suspend your beliefs around how hard and challenging your life has been. That may absolutely be true, but what if everything that has happened is *for* you—including all the difficulties, pain, and suffering—and has served you in some way to become stronger, more determined, and wiser?

If you can, accept what has happened, which does not mean you agree or condone it at all. Learn what you can from all of it and use it for your growth, not your demise, to help you be more understanding and compassionate. Share that compassion with yourself first, because you have suffered a lot. Then, share it with all others. The benefits to you are immense, and you contribute to happiness in the world.

Who Are You?

Who are you really—beyond your name and the roles you play? There are basically four different aspects of you: physical, emotional, mental, and spiritual. Who you are fundamentally is a Soul on a mission to learn and evolve your consciousness, to understand more about yourself and life, and ultimately to contribute to the evolution of the consciousness of the collective.

The Soul's Journey

As a Soul, we choose or are assigned a physical body as well as an emotional and mental body, all chosen for specific lessons and strengthening. Our soul indwells in this body for the duration of this lifetime on Planet Earth. We also choose our parents, siblings, and our circumstances.

You may well ask, *What was I thinking?* or simply experience gratitude. Sometimes souls choose difficult circumstances—not to sit in them and be defeated—but to experience the joy of overcoming them through finding themselves and a greater purpose that transforms the pain and suffering. Or someone may choose a wealthy background to discover that money isn't where happiness and peace of mind is.

Exercise

Be curious and wonder why you ended up with your particular family. What have you learned from the situation? What has been revealed to you?

No judgements, just reflections.

Journal about any insights you have.

We are all an individuated spark of the Creator, a fractal clothed in a body with a mind and emotions. We are in this vehicle with no operating instructions, a mind that drives us crazy, and emotions most of us have no idea how to process, so we ignore or avoid them. Then we are set forth into a world we don't understand and are expected to cope.

What if . . .

- it could be different?
- we could put ourselves back into the driver's seat?
- we could empower ourselves, heal, learn, grow, evolve, and create anew?

I believe we are meant to thrive. What do we need to do?

To be able to see through these times of massive and rapid change, we need to understand ourselves, who we are, what makes us tick, and how the different aspects of ourselves work and interact together for us to be able to show up more authentically.

How are you showing up? As your full powerful self or as a limited, diminished self?

Most of us are definitely not showing up in our full power as our True Selves because of the limiting stories we tell ourselves, which stem from our conditioning from the familial, cultural, and collective sources we have been immersed in.

The physical, emotional, and mental aspects of you make up your personality, how you express into the world. Your body is your vehicle through which you gather the necessary experiences you have agreed to and forgotten—thank goodness—for your learning, growth, and evolution to deepen your understanding of who you are: your strengths, growth edges, and what you are capable of being, doing, contributing, and receiving. This is your sacred work.

We will be exploring each aspect with suggestions on how you might bring each one individually and collectively into greater balance. They all work together to form you as a wholistic being. As you bring these parts into greater harmony, the magic begins to unleash the spiritual aspect of you, your True Self. Your intuition becomes your guidance system in the world, and you can truly source from your Heart, your strengths, and your unique ways of knowing.

The ideal is to bring the Heart and brain into coherence, combining the wisdom of the Heart with the intellect of the brain, to make the best choices to manifest your heartfelt desires.

CHAPTER 7

Tools of Consciousness

We evolve our consciousness through expanding our awareness by coming into the relational field. The common denominator at the basis of all the malaise on all levels we see in the world is *disconnection*. These tools will help you to come into right relationship and re-establish deep connection with yourself, your body, Nature, and life.

Becoming more aware of yourself as a multifaceted being brings greater understanding of who you are and begins to realign you with your Truth.

Direct yourself to become more conscious of your worldview, which includes:

- Your habits
- Your beliefs
- Your self-talk
- Who you believe yourself to be
- What you believe is your lot in life

Your worldview is critical and will soon reveal whether these basic beliefs support you or not. If they don't, then make different choices. Catch yourself in the act of thinking or expressing these aspects if you can and ask: *Is this really true? Does it serve me to keep believing this?*

It is critical that you develop the ability to notice a felt sense of *yes* and *no* in your body. Does something feel safe or unsafe, light or heavy or dark, good or bad? Is it a clear signal to move forward or stay back or pause for more information?

One of my mentors, Anna Reidenbach, speaks of the sacred *yes* and sovereign *no*. What are we saying yes to? What are we agreeing to? Is it serving us? Does it feel like a clear yes or a definite no? To learn about Anna Reidenbach, look for her in the Resources listed in the back of this book.

It is not always immediately clear; perhaps you will need to pause and sit with the question. At times, you might feel excitement or nervousness. These feelings could signal your comfort zone is about to be stretched for your learning and growth.

It is also good to note that sometimes on the other side of the sovereign no is a sacred yes. Be open. What might that be in your life? What could you stop agreeing with, in order to welcome in more love and peace and lift your consciousness?

This discernment is part of your personal navigation system as you deepen your intuition and your trust in it.

Practise and notice:

- What's the feeling?
- Name it.
- Where in your body do you feel it?

- Place your hand there to meet that aspect of yourself. What does that part need? Compassion, love, encouragement?

Neutral observation will deepen your skills. Stay out of judgement. Talk with your body. It listens to every word you say. Let it know you will be doing some different things, exploring and experimenting, in order to create a more satisfying reciprocal relationship.

I offer you some tools that guided and saved me from being stuck on the hamster wheel of repeating patterns of hurt, suffering, ultra-vigilance, strained nervous system, drama, and exhaustion. Situations are brought to us over and over to see if we can and will respond in a different way that may serve us better. We can learn something new by consciously creating new meaning about the situation, meaning that can free us instead of keeping us trapped in the repeat cycle. Then, we can move on, no longer needing to repeat that pattern.

As you work these techniques, they will reveal insights into the different aspects of yourself that you can utilise to grow and evolve. They tend to overlap each other as they work with you to move you forward. I hope that these practices are what gives you the new experiences that create a new reality for yourself. Otherwise, it is just untested information.

A wise saying often attributed to Carl Jung is:

I am not what has happened to me. I am what I choose to become.

This is your opportunity to choose who you become.

Personal Responsibility/Response-ability

You are the authority of your own life: your body, your thoughts, your beliefs, your behaviours, and the actions you take. Your thoughts and beliefs about yourself, others, and the world—and what you believe is or isn't possible in any of those categories, whether true or false—inform and contribute to creating your experiences in life and, therefore, your reality.

Accepting this Truth creates the ability to take 100 percent responsibility for what you have created in your life, albeit mostly as an unconscious creator as that's where most of us begin. I wonder what you will create in your world from now on as a conscious creator.

Where others are involved, take 100 percent responsibility for your part, active or passive. In circumstances beyond your control, take 100 percent responsibility for your internal responses to the situation. Sometimes, that is the only environment you can control.

You may need a lot of practice and kindness as you come face-to-face with old patterns. To truly move into mastering your life, you need to leave behind any sense of victimhood as it weakens you and makes you someone that life happens to, rather than someone who is consciously creating a life that works and a belief system that supports that.

Victim consciousness vibes at a much lower frequency. When you are a conscious co-creator, you become the *cause*, and your life becomes the *effect*. You lift your frequency higher; your perspective broadens. You are in the driver's seat. Granted, we have all been victims in life, and many circumstances are beyond our control, but it's our response, our interpretation, that shapes our reality.

When you take responsibility and do your inner work, these aspects become transformed and integrated into your being. You then feel more energised, whole, authentic, and more like yourself in ways you may not have experienced before, which gives you greater confidence in the world.

When we haven't done the work, these unresolved issues will drain our energy, block clear thinking, rev up the nervous system, and deplete us in every way. Your inner power is accessed as you begin to take responsibility for your life.

Adopt a Growth Mindset

A growth mindset is characterized by the following:

- Seeking different opportunities
- Entertaining multiple possibilities
- Adopting different perspectives
- Being honest with yourself
- Showing kindness to yourself
- Willingness to course-correct
- A belief that change is possible
- Choosing to respond positively rather than react negatively
- Looking for the growth opportunities in every situation

If we can change our minds about something we had perceived as negative and change the meaning we were making of that by going deeper with our exploration and interpretation, we grow our awareness, expand our consciousness, and lift our frequency. Ask: *What else is possible here?*

What if life happens *for* us rather than *to* us? What if it was always working in our favour to grow and evolve us to lead us in new directions with new understanding and motivation to do things differently? This perspective is absolutely essential for this journey.

I consider curiosity to be a superpower. It is a disrupter of the old patterns and a seeker of new possibilities. Nothing will change unless we get curious, ask different questions, and consider different viewpoints.

On the other hand, a fixed mindset is one in which change is not possible voluntarily, and a different way or a different point of view is not accepted nor explored. If we believe the same things we always have, do things the same way we always have, react to things the same way we always have, there is no growth, no flexibility, no other possibilities.

When we keep doing things the same way we always have, expecting a different result, we call that the definition of insanity. We think: *If I just work a little bit harder or love them more, they'll notice me and be nicer, like I did.* Is that working?

A fixed mindset keeps you stuck in the loop of old beliefs and perspectives, of repeating patterns, such as attracting the same kind of people or illnesses. Consider the possibility that you draw something to yourself in order to see it as another opportunity to act differently. You are meant to rise above that particular challenge.

In a growth mindset, a whole smorgasbord of new perspectives, interpretations, and meanings open up. Possibilities abound in a growth mindset; there is more spaciousness and creativity flows. You get to play and ponder with other options available for you.

In a fixed mindset, it's generally a one-lane highway to one response, one solution that may not be the best one. We justify our thoughts and actions righteously. If a course of action hasn't worked in the past, it's time to get creative and wonder what else is possible.

Just putting a question in the space, *What else is possible here?* opens up the energetic field of your mind and the greater field of consciousness to drop in a different possibility. Ask what meaning you are making here. Could there be a different, more empowering meaning you could make? Even seeing a challenging situation as an opportunity is an empowering thought. Be curious and creative.

Choosing Your Focus

What you focus on and put energy into is what you attract. It's the Law of Attraction. Focus on what you do want, not what you don't want. The vibe of your thoughts can attract similar vibes, so choose well. Otherwise, you could be amplifying what you don't want.

Always practice kindness towards yourself and accept that we all lose focus at times. As soon as you realise you're going down the wrong path, choose a different, more uplifting one.

Acceptance

When you come into acceptance—which does not mean agreement or condonement—you begin to cease *againstness*. You release the energy tied up in resistance, and you build a stronger internal foundation for your life. If something already *is*, there is no point denying or fighting it.

Work towards changing it by making wise choices to change the situation for yourself and possibly others. Often, I use the phrase, *It is as it is,* as a pattern interrupt, not a cop-out, to create space to accept the situation and introduce change. *This too shall pass* is also useful. Always embrace the learning opportunity present.

Acceptance allows you to stop and assess what's happened, to observe your emotions around that, to release judgements on self and others, and to create a different path forward. It begins with Self, as everything does, to accept all the different aspects of yourself, including the ones you would rather not own or reveal—such as being manipulative, selfish, dishonest, mean, disturbed, or lonely.

When you come into relationship with these parts of yourself to acknowledge, witness, listen to, and care for them, your whole world can change. You are giving them a voice, allowing their story and feelings to be heard and felt, which can then allow them to be transformed, healed, and integrated.

By ignoring or avoiding them, you allow the energy draining of their triggering and calling for your attention to continue unabated. You are also unwittingly shutting down your own voice.

We all want to be heard and seen. Are you willing to hear and see yourself?

It is a matter of accepting that something occurred in the past that you didn't have the skills to process and release at the time. You are now choosing to access your power to move on with your life towards greater health, happiness, and sanity.

Things happen that you can hopefully learn from and become wiser, stronger, clearer, and more compassionate towards yourself and others. You can then let go of the victim role and empower yourself to be all you can be.

Forgiveness

The simple act of forgiveness is not necessarily a religious act. Religions use it in their own way. It is such a powerful tool for dissolving the negativity in your mind and body. Forgiveness is a practice that can set you free from a lifetime of carrying guilt, shame, blame, and resentment, which are all expressions of unresolved issues. It can unravel stuck energy and free you up for thinking differently—getting you out of the repeat loop of old stories—and move you towards being more creative and getting on with your life.

Forgiveness is a sacred practice as it will take you deep into your core, your Truth.

It is really only yourself that you truly need to forgive:

- For holding judgements against yourself and others
- For holding on to anger, resentment, disappointment, grief, and more
- For creating discomfort, dysfunction, and possible disease in your body

The other people involved may become irrelevant as you will no longer be triggered.

Forgive yourself for any judgements against yourself for acts of hurt and anger you may have perpetrated. The energy of judgement remains inside you until you clear it. Judgement and guilt are big contributors to disease.

Forgiveness Exercise, Part 1

In a private space, say silently or out loud your own version of this statement:

I forgive myself for judging myself for being/doing/ believing/avoiding/holding on to _______, and I release it now for the highest good of all concerned.

Breathe in Light and let go of negativity on the outbreath. You need to be authentic and truly mean what you say. Saying the words and not really meaning them while still being invested in the judgement doesn't work.

Life responds to your intent, your frequency, and your beliefs. It's important that you find your own words that target the trapped energy in your body. Keep repeating this process, adding different wording and naming the feeling you are experiencing as you go deeper into the issue, until you know without a doubt that those limiting beliefs no longer run your life.

You will feel it in your body. This may take several sessions. I should add that some things may revisit, with lesser intensity, just to test your response.

Forgiveness Exercise, Part 2

Be patient, kind, and compassionate with yourself. This is a big deal. I like to complete the practice by adding:

I forgive myself for forgetting that I am a spiritual being having a human experience. (and/or) I forgive myself for forgetting that I am Divine.

These words will bring you into greater alignment with Truth. I used them regularly when I was going through my challenges. They helped enormously.

When you judge others, that judgement is stored in your body. Forgiving yourself for holding on to those judgements releases the other person from your energy field. And if you feel the need to forgive others involved, do so.

When you have deeply forgiven yourself, something magical happens—an energetic release of those thoughts, beliefs, judgements, and unresolved feelings that have been trapped in your body, for years perhaps, that do not serve you.

You can be liberated from the chains of conditioning and limiting beliefs that have resided in your subconscious, just below your conscious awareness. They have tended to run your responses to life, repeating emotional and mental patterns that have locked you into pain and grief. These old *stories* will drain your energy until you address and resolve them, freeing up that energy for you to create something new. It is that simple and powerful.

Then celebrate! Dance it out. Create a ceremony around honouring yourself and your courage for freeing your spirit.

Forgiveness Exercise, Part 3

At night when you get into bed, run through your day in your head and forgive yourself for any perceived wrongdoings. Clear them each day so they don't accumulate. Forgive yourself for judging yourself or others. You will feel lighter and sleep better.

When we stop using the intellect of the mind and come to the wisdom of the heart, we access the door to Divinity, because out of that heart comes the compassion and forgiveness.
—Hazrat Inayat Khan, Sufi mystic

Gratitude

The attitude of gratitude can help reset your energy and set you free. It can change your energy so quickly. When we focus on the things we are grateful for, the tight energy in our body dissipates.

Consider focusing on little things:

- You're still breathing
- Rest

- Shelter
- The warmth of the sun on your skin
- Flowers
- Sunrise and sunset
- The stars
- Uplifting music
- A cuppa of favourite tea/coffee/chai in a favourite mug

Anything. Play, get creative. Celebrate and utilise everything to express gratitude. It can become a light-hearted game to be grateful for the tiny things as well as big things, even difficult challenges as opportunities to grow, learn, and evolve.

Sometimes, we might not recognise blessings immediately. They can be disguised as hardships and blocked pathways. With hindsight, we can recognise that those times held some of our greatest learnings and often strengthened us and set us in new directions. In those times, we can say:

I am grateful for all the possible blessings in this situation that I may not be aware of yet.

These words leave our Hearts and minds open for new awareness to arrive.

When I first started practicing being grateful for challenges, the words were said with a good dose of sarcasm. My mind was saying, *Yeah, right!* But soon it made me laugh, which changed the energy and expanded my world.

Gratitude is a game changer. The simple act of saying, *I am grateful for all the blessings and gifts in my life* can take you to a new level of empowerment from which to start, reset, or end your day. Gratitude brings you into alignment with your True Self, the vibration of you in your Truth, and you can rest in that. The vibe of gratitude can attract more things to be grateful for. And so it goes on.

Appreciation is an expression of gratitude. Start with yourself for your beautiful Heart, your courage, and your sensitivity that allows you to come into compassion with others. Add anything else you can think of.

Appreciate others for any fine qualities you witness. Make their day. Always be appreciative for the beauty of Nature: the beautiful hills and plains, the waters, the flora and fauna, the sun and stars, planets, and constellations. Make it a habit to appreciate the things and people around you.

It's like Pollyanna's "Glad Game" (Porter 1913). It lifts your vibration and those around you. Gratitude is a high frequency emotion like love, joy, and happiness.

When my children were young, I started writing in five things in a gratitude journal that happened during the day that I was grateful for. Some days, all I could be grateful for was that I was finally in bed and still breathing, that we'd all been fed and had clean clothes to wear the next day. Other days, I could celebrate witnessing life's expression through my children or something good I had done that day.

I re-read those diaries over and over again in my down times, and they always lifted my spirits and made me smile in remembrance of some of the good times of the past.

There has been quite a bit of research into the practice of gratitude and its benefits for our health and happiness. Some findings include reducing depression and anxiety, increasing willpower, keeping your calm, and boosting morale (Schmoe 2020).

The really cool thing about gratitude practices—like writing in a diary or being thankful to ourselves and others–is they actually rewire the brain to adopt a self-perpetuating behaviour. You are cultivating a new habit; therefore, a new neural pathway is created to facilitate this.

Perhaps this could make us smarter as well. Mental health has many complexities, but for day-to-day wellbeing, the research clearly shows the cultivation and expression of genuine gratitude can make a huge difference. It can help lift you out of the ruts of confusion, hopelessness, and helplessness to knowing that you can do so much for yourself by yourself. You are the architect of your life.

Exercise

Start your own gratitude journal.

Choose a special one that uplifts your spirit, perhaps even one you have decorated yourself. It may be too much at first to do it every day or to write five things each time. Just start with what you can do and work up to increasing it.

Compassion

We can heal through compassion. When you bring compassion to yourself, shame can be healed. Most of us have carried shame, and it is a heavy burden. Being willing to practise self-compassion for all that you have endured, that may have kept you stuck in shaming stories you tell yourself, begins the healing. It softens and nourishes your inner being and allows you to move gently forwards.

Acknowledge yourself for all that you've been through. Remind yourself that it's no wonder you felt this way. You made the best choices you could at the time; you didn't understand.

It is so important that we allow ourselves to feel those feelings in a safe, accepting space. Cultivate the practice of holding space for those aspects of yourself—acknowledging, witnessing, and caring for that part of you that is expressing. You can also apologise for not always being present or willing to come into relationship with yourself for fear of what you might find. You could choose to do some forgiveness work around that. It's a deeply rewarding journey back to wholeness.

Self-acceptance > self-forgiveness > self-compassion > self-respect > self-appreciation > self-love.

It's all about mastering your energies—so important in these transitional times.

Offering compassion to others is a simple, beautiful, powerful gift—just being present, to hold space for them to speak, hearing their thoughts on their journey without judgement, without interruption. When they have finished their story, acknowledge that you can see or hear how hard that has been for them—*no wonder they felt bad*—and share what you see as their strengths. Everyone needs to be witnessed, to be heard and have their existence validated. Their frequency will lift and so will yours. It's a win/win.

Mindfulness

Being present in the moment brings your conscious attention to whatever you are doing, including eating, exercising, meditating, working, communicating, and more. The *now* moment is the only moment we can truly live, experiencing life, just being. Many of us tend to live in either the past, which can produce feelings of guilt or shame, or in the future, which can set us up for anxiety and worry as to what might happen. Mindfulness or being present is a way of connecting with yourself, your breath, and your Heart's yearnings while dreaming into new possibilities for your life. In the now moment, there is no space for past judgements or future worry.

Mindfulness is a prerequisite for deep relaxation, meditation, creativity, and healing. When you are eating, become present with the meal and notice the taste, the flavours: spicy, warm, nourishing, enlivening, calming. When outside, notice the light, the feeling of the sun or the wind on your skin, the smells, the beauty of nature, birdsong, or the colour of a flower, its shape and scent if any. When you focus on what you are doing, you are present, you are naming qualities, and you are out of the realm of the old stories and low frequency feelings like guilt, anger, fear. Your body is more relaxed, which is better for digestion and keeps the stress hormones at bay.

Language

Speak kindly to yourself. You deserve it. You have been through such a lot of challenging times. Speak kindly to others also. We don't know their journeys or what they are dealing with.

Train yourself to listen to what you tell yourself. Monitor your self-talk. It affects your energy, your frequency, your wellbeing, and your self-esteem. I remember deliberately tuning in to my thoughts one day years ago and recording the negative thoughts I had about myself, others, and life. I had an index card full of strikes by the end of the day, and they were only the ones I managed to catch in my awareness.

There was a dismal number of happy thoughts on the other side of the index card.

I experienced a stark realisation of what I was doing to myself without thinking about the impact, imprinting on myself constantly the energy of dissatisfaction, disappointment, frustration, resentment, lack, and more. I became more conscious and started changing my thoughts as soon as I was aware of them. I began intentionally choosing my focus.

Try it. Make it a game of awareness—no judgements, just encouragement as you course-correct. *It is as it is* until enough practice changes it to something else that can serve your health and happiness.

Talking negatively to yourself is a behavioural pattern, which, if allowed to continue, can create the domino effect of sending stress chemicals associated with negative thoughts circulating around your body. This, over time, can start causing inflammation and possibly set up conditions for chronic dis-ease.

Notice actual words you use, such as:

This is killing me.
I won't survive this.
This is destroying me.
My body is useless or ugly.
This is to die for, or to kill for.
I can't do this.
I'm not good enough.

It may seem innocuous, but your body consciousness is a loyal servant and takes quite literally what you say, think, and imagine. Its job is to serve, and it can begin creating what you have instructed it to do. Raise your awareness about what you are putting into motion. They are not only instructions to your body, but also to the Universe.

As mentioned before, research has shown that the brain cannot distinguish between real and imagined (Saplakoglu 2023). When we keep going over a traumatic situation that occurred, we are re-shocking our body, catapulting it back into the trauma, increasing stress chemicals in the body and angst and confusion in the mind. This creates a vicious circle that does not serve us.

Likewise, when you imagine what you deeply yearn for and do not yet have, wonder what that might look like and feel it in your body as though you already have it, so your energies can be directed towards creation. This focus charges the field so that you can more effectively draw it towards you. Make sure it is what you truly want to be, feel, see, and experience in your world, and that what you are focusing on can do no harm to yourself or another.

In particular, be aware that the words *I am* are extremely powerful and potent in all languages. In ancient texts, these words were believed to have the power of sixteen suns. This is hard to conceive, but it sounds incredibly powerful so be conscious of the words you put after them as they become amplified and can magnetise that energy to you.

Choose wisely and ensure the words you choose are positive and life-enhancing. For example, instead of saying, *I am unhappy and depressed,* try *I am experiencing something that feels like sadness and grief, until I can support myself to make a different choice.* It's good to acknowledge and honour those feelings, and when you're ready, choose a different focus.

I wonder what different choice you could make to uplift yourself. Remind yourself of all the good things you are and do: your kindness, your sense of humour, your spaghetti Bolognese. Anything.

This practice helps remove any label you may be identifying with and puts more space between the condition and you. It is not about who you are, but who you are being. The frequency of who you are being in that moment is broadcast into the field around you and can attract similar vibrations. Misery can attract misery.

Likewise, happiness or lightheartedness can attract more of the same. Focus on what you do want, not what you don't want. When who you are being is in alignment with who you are at your core, then the whole game of life changes.

This alignment is a growth edge for most of us and requires discipline and retraining the mind to support us in choosing something more empowering. Always practise patience and kindness with yourself as you readjust your way of being with yourself and in the world.

Exercise

Notice the difference in energy of these two phrases and how you respond to them:

1. Anti-war
2. Pro-peace

Some would think they are the same, but their energy and emphasis are different.

- Which one feels more comfortable for you to align with?
- Which one feels like a yes or a no?

Observe your energy. It's important to start tracking your internal responses to different things like words, people, food, events, ideas.

- Which ones make you feel good, or repel you?
- What makes you feel lighter inside or heavier, contracted or expanded?
- How can you use this feedback from your own body to make better choices for yourself?

Spend a few minutes twice a day, perhaps when you go to bed at night and before you get up in the morning, imagining, seeing, and feeling what it is like to have that which you desire in your life.

Realigning Your Energy Field

Some people, situations, or thoughts can make you feel drained. My teacher John-Roger taught his students this technique: To clear negativity from your energy field, place your hand on your forehead and say, *Clear, disengage, disconnect for the highest good through the highest Light/Source/Divine.* Say this or whatever works for you.

Breathe in and let go of the negativity on the outbreath. Always use the phrase *for the highest good.* We may think we know what is for the highest good, but we don't. We do not always know or understand our own Soul's journey, let alone another's.

It is also useful to notice when you're with other people if they energetically fill your cup or deplete it. Then, you can make choices on how much or if you want to spend time with them. Your life-force is precious. Protect it by making choices that serve you.

When you notice an uncomfortable feeling come into your awareness, you can ask: *Who does this belong to?* Don't look for an answer. It doesn't matter who it belongs to as long as it's not yours. An answer may drop in later, but don't waste your time waiting; otherwise, you may draw it back in by focussing on it. The energy should lift. I learned this technique from Dr. Dain Heer, Co-Founder of Access Consciousness (Heer 2024).

Research shows that approximately 95 percent of our thoughts are not our own (Tucker 2025). We pick them up energetically from others like psychic sponges (Lebow 2021).

We can be confused and think thoughts are our own. Ask the question given to me by Dr. Heer, and most times, it will dissipate, unless it is yours and there's deeper work to do.

Do your best to stay lighthearted. Be playful. If you are too serious or demanding, it might block the magic. It's all about the frequency you are being.

Neutrality

Practise neutrality to decrease your inclination to judge yourself or others. Do your best to notice when your mood changes—the drop in energy and the associated uncomfortable feelings—and go inward to find out what the drop is about and resolve it to the best of your ability on the spot.

Neutrality brings the great gift of pause. Take a breath, regulate your nervous system, and think before you speak. Being an observer gives you back control on how you handle what life brings. It takes practice—all new habits do—discipline, willingness to course-correct where needed, and self-love, knowing you are worth it.

Pausing gets easier and becomes a game, catching yourself just before you go into full flights of fancy or a rant. This moment brings in the Light and lightens up the mood. Celebrating any wins is a way of anchoring them into your body.

Witnessing Yourself

You are the life coach of the different aspects of yourself, your inner children who are triggered based on past experiences and want your attention to feel better. You will keep getting triggered until you resolve the source, using all the Tools of Consciousness above. Your inner children need to be witnessed—to feel heard, seen, and acknowledged—to know that they matter. They want to know you're there for them, that you won't abandon them, that they are loved no matter what. Just like any child. Or adult.

When we do our inner work, these aspects become transformed and integrated into our beings. We feel more energised, more whole, more like ourselves, giving us greater confidence in the world.

Meditation

Meditation is another spiritual practice that brings you into greater connection with yourself and with higher frequencies of existence, inspiration, understanding, peace, bliss, and oneness. It's a quiet practice of stillness with deep, slow, calm breathing that brings your focus away from the outside world into your inner world. Focusing on the breath will bring you into the present moment where the past and future don't exist. There are many online sources to find a meditation practice that suits you.

Here is a suggestion you could try.

Meditation Exercise

Close your eyes and come into silence and stillness, slowing and deepening your breathing.

Bring your attention into your body as you follow your breath down into your beautiful courageous Heart. Feel the energy of calm and flow, intelligence, aliveness, possibility, of creation.

Observe the energy going deeper into your body, into your torso, nestling between your hips, your creative centre.

Follow the energy down your legs and connect into Mother Earth. Offer your thanks for everything she provides for your life. Receive her blessings.

Allow that grounded energy to rise again into your creative centre.

Gather your resourcefulness up to the Heart to simply be and receive its wisdom.

Then allow your energy to expand beyond your body into the plasmic electric field that flows through us and around us. This is the creative manifesting field of unconditioned energy that we can source creative ideas from. Feel the peace and love in in the realm of possibilities. You may even receive some inspirational thoughts.

When you're ready, bring your awareness back into your body, breathe deeply, let it go, and open your eyes— rested, alert, and ready for what's next in your life. You can start with five minutes and build up to twenty minutes or more if you can feel the benefits.

Journal about any insights you may have gained.

Sacred Rituals and Ceremony

Create rituals and routines and beliefs that enable you to meet the sacred every day. Make a list of the things that bring you joy and put a smile on your face whenever you notice them. Let the list grow, and when feeling down, choose something from your list.

You can experience joy from things as simple as:

- Sun on your face
- Beautiful flowers
- Wearing a favourite shirt or scarf
- Listening to uplifting music
- Dancing
- Watching an inspiring movie
- A conversation with a friend or a stranger
- Tasty homemade food
- Fresh veggies in your garden or from the local farmer's market
- Happy children

Honour and celebrate the natural cycles of life. Pay attention to the moon phases, especially the new moon as an inner time to reflect on what you would like to attract in your life, being specific and descriptive. Set an intention. The full moon is a time for shining the Light on your desires, magnifying and amplifying them. Be curious about how you might create opportunities and action plans to do these.

Celebrate the solstices and equinoxes and notice the change of seasons, which can be accompanied by changes in food and changes in moods. Autumn and winter are usually times to go inwards to reflect, and spring and summer are seasons to be outside more, celebrating growth and new opportunities. Learn more rituals that foster connection to the magic of life.

Celebrate birthdays and anniversaries of significance in whatever way works for you, whether it be with loved ones or simply by yourself, honouring the magnificence of *you*.

Make time for yourself to do your chosen practices that support you to be strong, resilient, and resourceful. Make time for your family, relationships, and friends to strengthen bonds and mutual support. Choose priorities that serve you as best you can, so you can serve the world with your presence, your innate uniqueness, your kind nature, and beautiful Heart. We are all up to something big, and our energy and intention for life connects us all.

Be an invitation for others so they want to know more by showing up as your empowered Self, sourcing from your new story of being and becoming. Join other groups aligned with your values. Or create your own to dream together, vision together, create and build together.

Margaret Mead said:

Never doubt that a small group of thoughtful, committed citizens can change the world; indeed, it's the only thing that ever has.

CHAPTER 8

Your Body Is a Genius

We Can Heal Ourselves

Over the years, I have learned that as human beings we are way more powerful than we've been led to believe, capable of healing ourselves physically, emotionally, and mentally. Independent science is showing us we are capable of consciously self-regulating our body, mind, and emotions with simple easy techniques. Check out the brilliant work of Gregg Braden, Dr. Bruce Lipton, and Dr. Joe Dispenza, all scientists and thought leaders who teach in these areas.

We are not powerless, at the mercy of waiting for a cure from outside ourselves. We are all naturally wired for connection—to ourselves, others, Nature, and a higher power. We already have the inbuilt mechanism within us to do this. When we begin to build a relationship with our body, based on mutual trust and kindness, we begin to understand its needs better and are more willing to do what it takes to create reciprocity of serving each other, which can lead to greater healing.

When we bring our body, mind, and emotions into greater harmony and balance with each other, we feel more alive. When our thoughts, feelings, and actions are aligned, we can activate our goals and dreams for greater health, happiness, and fulfillment. We expand our awareness and lift our consciousness, and we allow more space for our True Self to emerge and express itself.

This is the fourth aspect of ourselves, our Spiritual Self, and the most powerful. We begin to move towards our vision, and our vision begins to move towards us.

To illustrate the power of our body's capacity to heal, I want to share a couple of incidents from my own life. I have not healed myself of cancer or any other major disease, but I have prevented it. Even though tests showed a cancer gene, my life practices have not allowed it to turn on and express. The following incidents are possibly minor but show what is possible when we allow the body to do its healing work.

Healing Journeys

Towards the end of 2020, I started noticing red patches on my face that, in a short time, spread to my neck, chest, even into my armpits, which was very painful. I had an angry rash over most of my body. When I first noticed the red patches, I turned to what I knew to be healing foods: fruits and vegetables, fresh juices, smoothies, salads, soups. However, the rash kept growing worse and worse, not healing at all.

I could have gone to see a doctor, received prescriptions for anti-inflammatory pills and lotions. These could have given me relief but would not have addressed the cause. I knew my body could heal itself. I needed to figure out what it needed for support in healing.

So, I needed to think about it differently. I knew the liver is the main detoxifier in the body. I also understood that if it wasn't coping with the level of toxins in the body, possibly from sluggish lymphatic system, it would dump on the skin in order to continue doing its job.

In Traditional Chinese Medicine (TCM), the liver is associated with the emotions of anger and resentment, and I had built up a lot of those feelings over the years. The skin is associated with grief and sadness, and I have also experienced a lot in my life from losing family members and the perceived loss of a good marriage.

These emotions were trapped in my body, and even though I had done so much work emotionally and mentally, I hadn't really addressed the physical level deeply. I knew I ate good healthy food, rarely drank alcohol, and avoided coffee as the caffeine seemed to give me heart palpitations. I had a positive mindset, was forever the optimist, and I had good supportive friends and a relationship that was healing.

I had also asked Spirit many times to help me release anything I no longer needed. I obviously wasn't clear on how that might happen more gracefully. Spirit chose this time to help me to release. I had tried everything I knew could work, but nothing did.

My condition grew worse. My whole body reacted to almost everything. My skin looked like a scald with total coverage of my upper body and patches on the lower body. It would swell up, blister, and exfoliate every few days. Many days, I had to vacuum the dry scales of skin from my bed, around it, and the bathroom.

The only thing that gave some relief was organic aloe vera gel and an organic calendula ointment without any preservatives.

I was lucky my local health food store could get them for me. I could only wear cotton near my skin, and eventually, I bought some organic cotton sheets. They felt heavenly. I hadn't realised the difference between conventional and organic cotton so palpably before.

I rarely went out unless I was between bouts. Eventually, an old friend saw my condition and recognised it was similar to what she had experienced in recent times. She had found a cookbook for foods with low salicylates and amines—natural chemicals in our food—and loaned it to me.

It was a very plain diet: potatoes, onions and garlic, brussels sprouts, and green beans. I could also have legumes, gluten-free grains like buckwheat and rice, and some chicken, for which I was grateful. I lost so much weight. I soon made up for it by finding the food my body could accept—lots of homemade dips, patties, soups, breads made from these few ingredients, and occasionally meat, giving my body time to heal without the triggering foods.

The foods I had considered healing were not appropriate at this time. My liver could not cope with the level of toxins these healing foods were trying to push out—past emotions, stress hormones, and whatever else was still trapped in my body. The liver has to process emotions and hormones as well as food and chemicals and more. Negative emotions create stress hormones in the body that affect the chemistry and, therefore, the biology of the body. I needed the plain food of low salicylates and amines to give my body a rest from reacting so it could respond with healing.

One day I could feel an ocean of tears wanting to express. I asked my husband to hold me, and the waves swamped me as I sobbed and sobbed, releasing the grief, the sadness, and any resentments I still held. It was awkward for him, but he kindly obliged. It was so healing to allow myself to witness and express those emotions as they released through my body. I also used the Tools of Consciousness to clear negativity from my body.

I talked to the swollen face in the mirror each day—kindly, lovingly, humorously—to nurture and reassure my inner child that we would be okay. Eating the non-inflammatory foods, acknowledging and releasing emotions allowed my skin to heal after three to four months of endurance. My condition gradually improved over the next month or two.

Now, I can eat anything I choose, even spicy foods. I am so grateful I could trust my amazing body to do its job of healing itself and that I found the foods to support its journey.

My understanding now is that my body's internal environment was no longer a match for the new identity I had adopted as a powerful creator, worthy of love. I began with self-love and no longer saw myself as a victim. My body was aligning with this new way of valuing myself and life, my new story, and my new higher frequency.

Another revealing incident occurred when I dropped a heavy rubber-backed outdoor mat on its side straight across my big toe near the nail bed. I could feel my body revving up to receive the pain I knew was coming. I had this extraordinary thought which interrupted the process, *I wonder if I need to feel this pain.* The incoming pain stopped immediately even though I knew I had likely severed my nail. There was no pain, no bruising. It eventually healed, and the old toenail dropped off without any drama or pain.

These examples illustrate the power of the body to heal itself using the directed mind, a supportive environment, and appropriate foods on a foundation of self-love and self-belief to influence the desired outcome.

Your Body Is a Conscious Being

Your body is not only extraordinarily intelligent but is a conscious being. It has its own consciousness. According to Dr. Joe Dispenza, our bodies have over fifty trillion cells. Just imagine those trillions of conscious cells all working together and communicating through chemical and electrical signals to keep you performing the best you can, based on the fuel and environment you provide, both internal and external.

It's an amazing example of cooperation in a conscious community. They all know their unique job and carry it out in concert with every other cell, tissue, organ, and gland in the body. These trillions of cells are all listening to what you are saying to yourself. Are your words kind? Are they appreciative of the magnificent job your body does for you? Regardless of what you do or don't do, your body continues to do its best to keep you alive, until it can't any longer (Gustafson 2017).

When we are out of alignment physically, mentally, or emotionally, we feel it as discomfort. If the misalignment is more severe, we might call these effects *symptoms*.

Your body will try to get your attention through sensations, symptoms, and illness if you don't look after it. Symptoms are messages from the body that something you are doing or not doing is out of alignment with the integrity of your body/mind system and your path in this life.

Your body is your sacred vessel to care for and support so it can provide you with the energy and vitality you want to live your best life. That was the sacred contract you undertook before coming into your body.

How well are you performing your part? Bluntly, you need to serve your body first, your plans come second. You then have the energy and health to pursue your plans. It is meant to be a reciprocal relationship in service to each other. Your body can become your new best friend.

Exercise

Here are some reflection questions for you to ponder:

- What are you putting into your body and on your skin?
- Is it serving your body's vitality?
- Are you giving your body positive messages?
- Do you self-support or self-sabotage?

Journal any insights you gain.

We Are Made of Microorganisms

Science has found that we actually have more microbes than human cells (Shayne 2020).

Interesting thought! And these microbes have consciousness as well. They know precisely what their unique jobs are—their relationship with the specific part of your body they interact with—and they help keep you alive. They are essential.

For example, bacteria in the gut, called the *microbiome,* make up the majority of your immune system. These microbes are crucial in optimal digestion of your food.

We tend to believe that bacteria are bad, causing infections, but not all bacteria are bad. Antibiotics kill all bacteria, good and bad. If you take them, you will need to recolonise your gut with good bacteria from probiotics and prebiotics. You can buy capsules or ingest these through time-honoured practices of consuming cultured vegetables and fermented drinks, such as kefir and kombucha, which you can buy from health food shops or make yourself. It takes time and patience.

Science has also discovered a strong relationship between a healthy microbiome and good brain health. A healthy gut helps reduce depression and anxiety and improve mood due to the role the microbes play in production of certain hormones, such as serotonin.

Alkaline versus Acidic Diet

In the 1920s, scientist Otto Heinrich Warburg, Nobel Prize winner in 1931, discovered that healthy cells thrive in an alkaline environment full of oxygen. Conversely, tumour cells live in an acidic environment with low oxygen. They are anaerobic and do not survive in the presence of high concentrations of oxygen. Acidity is caused by highly processed diets with high sugar, physical inactivity, and emotional and mental stress (Urbano 2021).

Foods that acidify the body are refined sugar and derivatives and artificial sweeteners. There are no proteins, fats, vitamins or minerals in these food items, only refined carbohydrates that can harm the pancreas. Meat and products of animal origin—milk, cream, cheese, yoghurt, ice cream, eggs, and goat's cheese—are less acidic. Refined flour and derivatives, bread, margarine (fake butter), caffeine, alcohol, and cigarettes all acidify the body.

Foods that alkalise are all raw vegetables and fruits, almonds, chia and sesame seeds, and millet, an alkalising grain high in B17, a cancer-inhibiting vitamin. Other alkalising grains are amaranth and quinoa. Legumes, other nuts, and seeds can become more alkaline if soaked and sprouted. Real honey and green plants that contain chlorophyll are also alkalising.

A 60–80 percent alkaline and 20–40 percent acidic diet is usually recommended. Exercise helps oxygenate the whole body (Bridgeford 2024). A sedentary lifestyle creates issues in all areas.

Germ Theory versus Terrain Theory

The germ theory presented by the chemist Louis Pasteur in the 1800s was lauded as a great discovery and considered the most logical explanation for much illness and disease. This theory was supported by the new pharmaceutical industry started by the Rockefeller Foundation and Carnegie Foundation as an investment opportunity. They set about making products that battled germs.

The medical industry is now a multi-trillion-dollar industry. This fact supports a common criticism of this model: *health is bad for business.* To grow a business, you need repeat customers.

A contemporary of Pasteur's, Antoine Beauchamp, had a different idea called the *terrain theory*. He said it was the terrain—our inner and outer environment and the lifestyle choices we make to support both—that informs our health. Pasteur's theory was supported by the medical industry.

Think about it. One theory demands personal responsibility for our choices to support a healthy body and mind; the other relies on pharmaceutical products.

In our culture, we tend to talk about battles against bacteria or war against cancer and other diseases. Disease statistics are spiralling out of control, with cancer projected to affect one in two people. Diabetes is exploding, and cardiovascular disease is on the rise as is Alzheimer's disease. Many of our young people are heading towards obesity and chronic disease with growing numbers suffering from neurological disorders.

Despite billions of dollars being allocated to research, we are sicker as a society than ever. This money is usually spent on creating more testing equipment and more drugs, not on prevention or studying the cause and remedying those issues. Sickness management is a multibillion-dollar industry. The modus operandi is to treat the symptoms and ignore the causes.

We are physically and mentally burdened because of the toxic culture and environment we live in and because we haven't understood how to look after ourselves. We have been encouraged to hand over our responsibility for our own health to an *expert* who has studied *disease* for six or more years.

How much do medical practitioners learn about *health*? Apparently, very little in all those years. Fortunately, quite a few doctors have done extra studies on nutrition, acupuncture, meditation, and more, creating a more integrative style of medicine. Much is changing in that arena.

What if we could introduce a mindset shift from a disease sufferer and battler, even though it may look and feel like that, to *journeying* with the disease? This shift creates space between the disease and you. You are not the disease nor the victim of it, but a *journeyer* to learn what it has to teach you about yourself and life.

Ponder what choices may have led you there, and what other choices may lead you out. It will help you strengthen your resilience and claim your co-creatorship with life. There is a need for you to be proactive in seeking new ways in conscious co-creation, in choosing, researching, and experimenting with different remedies and protocols, different practitioners perhaps. Check the Resources List and research new ones.

To prevent illness and disease, and in many cases reverse disease, there is much we can do for ourselves by learning new ways and making different choices.

Epigenetics

Epigenetics, a relatively new science, tells us that genes do not dictate our health destiny, but they may give us a predisposition to certain diseases. Epigenetics means *above* genes or *beyond* genes. Dr. Bruce Lipton, a cellular biologist, says genes have less than 10 percent—and more likely 1 percent—influence, and that it is our environment, our perceptions of our environment, and our lifestyle choices that promote our health (Gustafson 2017). This supports the Terrain Theory.

If we follow the same diet, behaviours, and beliefs of relatives who have had a particular disease, that could heighten our predisposition. This new research creates new perspectives on all those things. We have the capacity to change our environment and our perceptions of it. If we subscribe to the genetic control theory, we become victims of our genes as the body will translate that belief into the chemistry and biology of our bodies (Lipton 2005). If we are open to epigenetic control, we then become the architects of enhancing our health.

This new science can empower you to take charge of your life.

As mentioned earlier in my story, my two older sisters were both diagnosed with cancer at thirty-three years old. As I approached thirty-three, I knew my mother was understandably nervous and worried. I simply told her cancer was not my journey. I knew I had a different life path. My lifestyle, diet, mindset, beliefs, and habits—my inputs were already different than my sisters'.

A month before I turned thirty-three, I found the spiritual teachings that became the foundation of my life. They have served me well to keep me happy, healthy, and resilient. These experiences support the epigenetic control theory and the Terrain theory.

Cancer Gene

Fifteen years later, I decided to be tested for the gene my two sisters had, which had been suggested to me a few times as the *responsible* thing to do. I was stunned and shocked to learn I had the same gene. The news was delivered in a way that made me feel as if I was a ticking time bomb.

The news was devastating. I barely slept that night and awoke the next morning with the thought that if I had lived an extra fifteen years, I must be doing something right. I decided to keep doing those things and researched more practices to incorporate into my lifestyle. That choice shifted everything. The doom energy dissipated, and a new journey with new awareness began. I changed my perspective and got a different result, which also supports the epigenetic control theory.

What Is Truly Needed for Radiant Health?

The ancient principles of health were taught to me mostly by Don Tolman who spent many years living with the people still using them and much of his life researching and teaching. All of these principles are now being backed by science, whereas in the past, he was considered too different and possibly threatening to the accepted knowledge of the time.

His studies show we need:

- Air
- Light
- Water
- Whole foods
- Movement
- Supportive relationships
- Passion

I have added:

- Earthing
- Nature
- Rest and stillness
- Social connection
- Creativity and fun

The people who reside in the *blue zones* of the world, such as Sardinia, Ikaria, Loma Linda, and Okinawa, are characterised by happy, healthy long lives and incorporate most of these principles into their daily lives. Many studies have been done on these groups and other cohorts, and interestingly, some show that while diet and exercise are significant, having a purpose in life, social connection, and a connection to something greater than ourselves is even more important. These things make our lives more meaningful.

Your body communicates to you all the time through sensations, comfortable or uncomfortable, and through feelings from anger to joy as a feedback mechanism for the choice to do more or less of an action or way of thinking.

We experience our world through our senses of touch, hearing, seeing, taste, smell, and our feelings. Many of us are remembering, developing, and utilising our intuition more and more. Our different ways of knowing need to be honoured and valued after centuries of ridicule and condemnation instead of relying only on the intellect. In these times we are living through, it is our intuition and Heart's wisdom that will see us through, because the mind solely will not be able to make sense of the things happening.

Many ancient and Indigenous cultures have known that all life is sacred. They understood the land is their mother, and as custodians, they have cared for and honoured her. Mother Earth has a consciousness, called *Gaia* by some. She provides for all our needs—physically, mentally, and emotionally. Your body is formed from the elements of her body. She knows your footprint and can tune in to your body and mind to help restore balance. Therefore, ancient wisdom understood the body as sacred.

The ancient Egyptian healers called the alimentary canal from mouth to anus the *river of life* or the *river of death*, depending on how clean it was. Our bodies are essentially a bunch of tubes from the heart, lungs, bones, and more. We need to keep them clear, to vent any blockages to prevent disease. The body does this through vomiting, diarrhea, copious mucus, and through the skin and fever. These are all intelligent natural responses of the body to rid itself of pathogens. They are uncomfortable but allow the body to do its job.

Note: Of course, if any of these functions become extreme, you may need to seek assistance from a trained professional.

They also believed that there are two causes of disease: deficient nutrition and excessive toxicity. I believe it is now a combination of both as more and more highly refined, processed food with synthetic additives—marketed as safe and convenient—are in the supermarkets as are many thousands of chemicals in our environment.

Perhaps studies into the cumulative effects of all these chemicals in our bodies and world would be useful. I believe the regulating agencies for food manufacturing have been captured by the industries they are supposed to be regulating. It seems to me there is less concern for safety and healthy ingredients and concern for only looks, taste, and profits. Sophisticated marketing can sell anything—unless we hone our critical thinking skills and do some research.

Coming into right relationship with your body and Nature is part of the sacred work you are here to do. Your body is your holy temple for this life, and it is your responsibility to care for it, to keep it in wholeness and holiness so it can thrive. Otherwise, you could be led to no life. To function at its best, your body needs the right fuel and the right environment where no harm will come to it. We will discuss these in the pages ahead.

Consider your body as your vehicle, like a car. You are the caretaker/driver, and you would not dream of putting orange juice or milk in a car's tank to fuel it. You would give it the oil-derived fuel it was designed to use.

Your body is designed to be fuelled from the natural world in which it evolved. Tuning in to the properties of Nature can feed, heal, protect, soothe, and inspire us. We can then add spiritual practices to grow our awareness, expand our consciousness, and come into greater balance and attunement to Life.

Regrettably, most of our natural systems have been compromised through ignorance, arrogance, corruption, and greed. Our air, water, and soils have become polluted by toxic substances. There has been little political will to change those practices. I truly believe that mighty Mother Nature can restore herself, but it will take cooperation from all of us to cease exploitative, rapacious, pollutive practices we have used and still use. Better choices can be made, and it starts with us questioning what we are supporting by how we spend our money. We can assist by understanding the essential integrity of Nature—and what she needs to maintain it—and how vital her balance is to our health and wellbeing.

Pollution is a major problem that needs to be tackled as soon as possible. I believe it is a bigger issue than carbon in the atmosphere.

Air

The breath of Life inspires us with our first breath and expires us with our last breath. It brings in the Spirit or the Soul, our lifeforce essence, for the duration of our lives and sets it free when we are done with this particular journey.

We are foremost electrical beings. According to Don Tolman, electricity is what keeps us alive. The greatest source of electric current is moving air. Air can become stagnant and electrically dead.

Sometimes air in air-conditioned buildings can become a bit stuffy and stagnant, and we can feel a bit drowsy or get headaches. Going outside in fresh air can help, so can more water to hydrate the body and brain. We can circulate air in our homes and electrify it by opening windows for about twenty minutes or use fans to circulate it.

Not only does inhaling bring oxygen into our bodies, but breathing consciously can regulate our nervous system by switching from the sympathetic nervous system of fight- flight-freeze into the parasympathetic nervous system that calms the body into rest and digestion support.

It's hard to relax when we are stressed. You could try this simple practice.

Exercise

Bring your attention into your body.
Focus on your breath. Slow it down and breathe deeper if you can.
Breathe in for five counts, hold for five counts, breathe out for five, and hold it out for five counts.

Do this five times. It can set up your day or reset it in stressful situations.

It has been suggested the longer you can hold the breath out before the next breath, the more beneficial the practice will be as it builds lung capacity and facilitates the interchange of the gases oxygen and carbon dioxide more easily. It is a powerful, simple, free practice that you can utilise to regulate your body.

There are many sources and variations of breathing techniques online. YouTube is a good place to look. Check out suggestions in the Resources at the end of the book.

Light

Light is information received by life on Planet Earth to activate energy and growth so that individual species may become what they are meant to be. The seeds in the ground are activated by the sun; life is stirred, and growth is promoted. An acorn is destined to become the oak tree, the seed from a gum tree is destined to become a gum tree, the rose seed, a rose. The acorn or seed holds the potential of the mighty oak, majestic gum, or exquisite rose within it.

Nature does not question what it is to become. This is to me a source for awe and wonder. We also have seeds of our potential to become our True Self. That voice that whispers to us of what we yearn for is in our Heart. It is the voice that tells us who we are designed and destined to be. Be aware that these whispers that speak of things not yet here are unique for each person. We will begin to reveal more of our True Self as we introduce more sacred self-care physically, emotionally, mentally, and spiritually.

If Light is information, we are receiving a lot of information from the sun, which is extremely active with many powerful solar flares in recent times. Earth's magnetic field has also dropped considerably, allowing radiation from far beyond our solar system from the galaxy to arrive here. This radiation also influences us, though in ways not many understand. Perhaps it is helping us to become more aware of ourselves, each other, our world, and beyond.

The sun interacts with our body in creating vitamin D. Most of us notice that we feel better in the sun. Feeling sunlight on our skin can make us feel happier. Vitamin D encourages the happy hormones and is crucial in serotonin production. There are now whole populations of people with chronic vitamin D deficiency, which can be a contributing factor to a number of diseases, such as diabetes, heart disease, cancer, osteoporosis, depression, and anxiety.

During the 1970s, we were conditioned to fear the sun, and it was demonised. Skin cancer was blamed on the sun. We need to also consider diets deficient in true nutrition and toxic ingredients in cheap sunscreens that can become carcinogenic with added heat, like the sun.

Research the ingredients; source the best you can afford. Talk to health food shop people who may offer some good advice. It is your responsibility to stay out of the sun at the hottest time of the day or wear a large hat and natural fibre shirt—cotton or linen—and use safe sunscreen if exposure is extended. Twenty minutes in the sun can give us the vitamin D we need, or you may take a good quality vitamin D3 plus K2 capsules or spray, especially in winter.

Water

Ancient Egyptian healers called water liquid sunlight. It also carries information and memory. Latest research is showing evidence of water having consciousness. This is not surprising as all life in the Universe is conscious, and everything is interconnected. What an extraordinary world and Universe we are living in! We are 70 percent water by volume, like Planet Earth, and 99.9 percent of our molecules are water molecules (Young 2022).

If water is conscious, are we speaking kindly? Are we thinking positively? Are we grateful for it and for life?

Amazingly, we are like bags of water that keep everything hydrated and flushing out toxins.

Replenishing good water daily through filtered, structured water and high quality, watery fruits is pivotal to our health. Coffee is a short-term stimulant and a diuretic, so limit yourself to one or two cups a day of the best quality, or better still, keep reducing until you drink none. Soft drinks have no life-force to offer your body. Eight glasses of water are suggested by most people. Do the best you can to gradually increase your intake if you are drinking less than that. Buy the best filter you can afford, and if you can't, bless each glass of water you drink with gratitude. It absolutely makes a difference in the quality.

Healthy water also holds electrical current through movement, like bubbling water from springs or fountains, rain falling from the sky, or streams bouncing off rocks and banks. The electrical current is what allows the cells in your body to be hydrated. At the very least, shake your water in a bottle, preferably a glass one, not plastic, to create that movement. Plastic chemical molecules like BPA can breakdown in sunlight and leach into the water in the bottle.

A Japanese scientist named Masaru Emoto experimented with water. He took samples from clean, structured water found in a remote forest and some from polluted water. He put drops on slides and froze them. He found the pure water made exquisite, beautiful crystals, and the polluted water was unstructured and irregular (Emoto 2001).

Another experiment was conducted at a polluted lake. Samples were taken from it before monks prayed over it and after. A non-structured blob of polluted water was transmuted and transformed into a beautiful crystalline structure. Breathtaking. Our thoughts, feelings, and intentions influence the water inside and outside of us. They can make the water more coherent or less, which internally can affect our health. Think what we could do to restore our waters, rivers, lakes, and even the oceans. There will be other technology as well in the near future to support that intention, using frequency.

There will be much more information coming out about the consciousness of water, its interaction with us, and what we can learn from it. It is said that water has come to us from meteors from other places in space. If it holds memory, what could it teach us?

There are also vast supplies of what is called *primary water* deep under the Earth's mantle. It is pristine, untainted water, a rarity on the surface of the Earth that perhaps can be a source in the future if needed. We might need a different technology, unfettered by corporate ownership, to access that.

Whole Foods

Whole means complete, not fragmented—nothing taken out and nothing added in. Industrialised, processed food is what most people eat as most don't grow their own food. Part of the process in manufacturing food items seems to entail taking out the good stuff and replacing it with artificial vitamins, preservatives, colourings, and flavours. These are synthetic chemicals that are not recognised by the body and can harm our balance.

Imagine the body as a biological computer. Whole foods have complete barcodes, while processed foods have barcodes with bits deleted and new ones added. The cells recognise the whole food barcode and know how to carry out the instructions. The body might be challenged by the manipulated barcodes, especially over time, and could begin moving from a lack of ease to dis-ease. Whole foods also hold intelligence from sunlight and the water process called *photosynthesis*. They hold information of repair, cleansing, healing, and building health for our cells.

Hippocrates said:

Let food be thy medicine and medicine be thy food.

It is important to connect with your food, to remember yourself as part of Nature, not separate from it, as defined in the dictionary. You can rekindle this relationship with your body, Mother Nature, and your food, noticing what different foods feel like in your body. This opens the lines of communication as you listen and notice and respond.

Does a food make you feel more alive, or heavy and dim?

A plant-based meal fresh from the garden or local grower has more life-force energy in it, because it was recently connected to the Earth. This energy passes on to your body for its optimum functioning, bringing more energy and more joy. It is part of the human experience to foster this connection. The more plant food in your body, the better.

A simple gratitude prayer over your food before eating can change the whole dynamic interaction between your body and food. You could try, *Bless this food and the people who brought it to me. Bless their families and work they do. I am grateful.* Or your own version. Blessing situations and things is not necessarily a religious practice, although it is used in religion. We all have the ability to be that which grounds the blessing in this world. It is part of our Divine nature. Use it with clear intention. Remember your body is your sacred vessel. It needs to be honoured and treated respectfully.

Source the best food you can afford. Grow your own or some of it, like herbs or nutritious sprouts. Buy local, seasonal, and organic if possible. Fast food, while it may seem convenient at the time, offers little to nourish your body. It is not a treat and should not be seen in this manner. If you get sick from lack of true nutrition, it is not convenient at all.

What you put in your mouth matters. It affects your energy, how you feel, your moods, and your ability to attune to yourself and to life. There is a connection between food, gut, healthy bacteria, and our brain. Lower rates of healthy bacteria in the gut can affect our moods and mental health.

The forces that made the body can heal the body. Whole foods provide an essential part of what our body needs to heal and maintain wellbeing. Proper nutrition helps work towards preventing or slowing any disease, reversing it, and eliminating it. It is possible to reverse many, if not all diseases. It takes work, commitment, a wholistic viewpoint, and seeking support from practitioners who know how to heal the body naturally.

There are many online summits with different experts offering their guidelines to healing disease that you can access to gain more understanding. See Resources.

Complex carbohydrates found in vegetables, fruit, some nuts and seeds, and gluten-free grains, such as quinoa, buckwheat, and amaranth, support brain health and the feel-good neurotransmitters. They also help balance our sleep-wake cycle and stoke the energy for our bodies. Refined carbohydrates found in processed, humanmade foods typically contain a lot of refined sugar, like cheap high-fructose corn syrup and refined white flour, which can contribute to blood sugar spikes and insulin insensitivity. These instabilities can exhaust the pancreas and degrade brain and body health overall.

Avoid gluten where possible; it can contribute to inflammation and impact neurotransmitter production in the gut and brain. It may also affect the thyroid that regulates hormones, which, in turn, may cause hormonal imbalance. Caffeine is a stimulant and may give you a bit of an energy rush, but overconsumption could contribute to adrenal burnout and exhaustion and could induce nervousness, anxiety, or depression.

Another magic thing about plants is that often the plant will have a part that shows us what it is good for in the body. This is called the *Doctrine of Signatures* and dates back to Hippocratic medicine. For example, a coconut looks like a hairy skull, and its fatty flesh is very good for the brain. Walnuts have a shell that looks like a cranium, encasing two wrinkly hemispheres They have good fat content that supports brain health. Kidney beans mimic the shape of kidneys and support renal health. Tomatoes are red with four chambers and are good for the heart. Red grapes are good for red blood cells, and white grapes are good for white cells. Figs are good for testicles.

Pomegranates are good for ovaries, heart, and circulation. According to Sayer Ji, founder of GreenMedInfo, pomegranates are the most hormonally regenerative fruit on Earth, and he shows they support not only women's health but men's testosterone levels and sperm quality—a miracle food much needed in these times of plummeting fertility in both sexes (Ji 2025). Avocados cut in half look like a womb holding a baby. They can help support the baby in utero and apparently are good for facilitating easier births.

A couple of myths that have been accepted for decades can be questioned: no salt and low-fat diets. Salt is essential for the body, but it must be good quality sea salt in moderate quantities. Sea salt has at least eighty-two different minerals that serve the body (82 Minerals 2024). I begin each day with two glasses of water with fresh lemon juice and a pinch of sea salt to support electrolyte levels in my body.

On the farm, I remember big blocks of sea salt on poles in the paddocks for the cows to lick when they knew their system was out of balance. Animals can be much smarter than humans. Table salt is highly processed and only has two different minerals that contribute to imbalance, so avoid that.

Fat is essential for all cell membranes, and our brain has a high content of fatty tissues. Eating good fats like coconut oil, avocados, nuts, seeds, and untainted, wild-caught, oily fish assists the quality of our cell membranes, improving brain and heart health. Good quality oils, such as olive oil and ghee also help. Make sure oil is not packaged in plastic. Glass bottles are best. Low-fat products are fairly tasteless, so there will usually be added sugar and flavours. It is processed food with the good stuff taken out and sugar, flavours, and preservatives often added.

We need to reduce our sugar consumption. Obesity is now a big problem, particularly in western countries. Processed foods, soft drinks, energy drinks, often with artificial sweeteners, such as aspartame can cross the blood-brain barrier. We do not want that in our brain. Lack of water and exercise can also contribute. Low self-esteem and negative self-beliefs also influence the performance of the body.

There may be other reasons, too, but those mentioned can be changed by making different choices about what you take into your body, including negative thinking about yourself.

Movement

Regular movement, such as walking, is a healthy practice to enliven your system. According to Don Tolman, we do cross patterning when walking, which is an alternate left leg/right arm and right leg/left arm action step by step. This movement electrifies your whole body and helps strengthen and cleanse. Perspiration also helps us cleanse. Cross patterning aids whole brain function and improves learning and memory.

Our lymphatic system requires movement to activate it. Movement improves our immune system, circulation, breathing, and so much more. Even micro movements can help—twirling our feet and hands, scrunching fingers and toes, flexing our feet and hands—especially if circulation is poor. It's amazing how this can kick-start our energy.

Yoga, tai chi, swimming, dancing, bike riding, running, and gym sessions are all good ways to keep our systems running smoothly for a happy, healthy, long life. You can combine a number of these principles by walking in the sun, breathing fresh air, and drinking some good water. Walk with a friend to foster social connection for twenty to forty minutes a day, or even five minutes is better than none. Do your best to facilitate your best health and best life.

Supportive Relationships

It makes sense that we feel happier, relaxed, energised, and inspired in healthy, mutually supportive relationships in which we feel seen, heard, and appreciated. Toxic relationships in which we feel criticised and not nurtured drain our life force through stress, worry, and loneliness, and over time, we can get very sick. Choose your friends wisely. Choose to partner with someone you can be best friends with. Happy supportive relationships can enhance everything about us.

Passion

Passion keeps us vital and sparks creative energy. It gives us a reason to get up and go. Passion is exciting, enlivening, and can influence others around us to feel it. Passion can be for anything you love and enjoy, from dancing to all creative projects—and obviously includes mutually good sex. Passion for life gives us purpose.

Earthing

Mother Earth is one big ball of healing negative electrons. When we connect our bare feet to the earth, grass, or sand at the beach, we draw up electrical energy that can energise us and reset our biological clock. Placing our bare feet on the Earth can put us in the time zone of wherever we are in the world. It grounds us and drains out the positive ions picked up from electronic devices and even synthetic clothing, which can be absorbed into the skin. Wear natural fibres as much as possible. The Earth takes the positive ions and feeds in the negative ions that can reduce inflammation, regulate our nervous system, improve clarity, and help keep us healthy.

Nature

Nature and everything she offers is one of the most powerful healers. If we can tune in to our body, environment, and Nature, we will find they speak to us all the time. Life is communicating to and through you, and inspiration is all around us. We can learn so much if we remain open and curious.

We initially evolved in a symbiotic relationship with Mother Nature. As a collective, we have strayed from that relationship. A loving reciprocity is possible with Nature if we appreciate her with our attention, respect, gratitude, and care through kind, sustainable practices. Celebration through ceremony and ritual is an expression of honouring her gifts. In turn, she provides us with all the elements needed for a healthy body, sound mind, and an abundant life.

We have come to understand that there is an energy transfer that is healing for us. In Japan, they practise forest bathing—immersing in Nature, being quiet and receptive. This type of practice soothes our frazzled nervous system, takes us out of flight-fight-or-freeze automatic responses to stress, and allows us to ground, relax, breathe, meditate, tune in, reflect upon, dream, visualise, and create.

Plants have an incredible intelligence. Through an alchemical process called photosynthesis, they convert sunlight and water to starches in order to grow and provide food and other resources for us. The byproduct of this process is oxygen, which allows life to exist on Earth. Crucially, plants take up carbon dioxide and sequester that into the soil.

All life on Earth is carbon-based. Carbon is essential, and we could solve or at least alleviate any *carbon crisis* by preserving natural environments, planting more trees, and stopping the clear-cutting of timber—a much simpler solution than some convoluted system of carbon taxes, credits, trading, and offsets. Or the ludicrous practice of banning farming and burying trees. I kid you not. Unfortunately. Who dreams up these things, and who benefits?

Get yourself out into Nature—the beach, a forest, a park or your backyard if you have one—pause, breathe deeply, and allow your nervous system to be comforted and regulated by the forces of Nature. She can work miracles.

Rest and Stillness

Adequate sleep is necessary for the body to rest, reset the nervous system, digest and prepare for elimination in the morning, repair, renew, and heal. Eight hours each night is the usual suggested quantity. You may need more or less to function well. See what works for you. If we do not get enough sleep, our energy diminishes, our immune system is lowered, and generally we can become very grumpy. Do your best to unplug from electronic devices an hour before bedtime. Read a book, listen to relaxing music, or engage in a fairly passive activity.

Stillness is like a meditation, resetting the nervous system, giving ourselves a chance to get out of our heads and just be, relax, tune inwards, daydream, wonder, ponder—generally taking space for ourselves. Find at least five minutes a day to practise stillness as often as possible. Be in Nature or somewhere quiet. Relax. Breathe.

Social Connection

It is important to have social contact with others, particularly like-minded, like-hearted people. Loneliness can drain our life force and makes life more meaningless. Seek connection. Join groups in whatever your interests are from hiking or cooking to car clubs, book clubs, or learning a language. Think about what your interests are and find a group or start one.

Creativity and Fun

Being creative keeps the energy flowing in our body. Whether it be music, dancing, painting, sewing, cooking, woodworking, gardening, writing poetry, or storytelling—whatever brings you joy—we often have a vision in mind that we can express through those media, which gives us pleasure. Pleasure is so good for our bodies and minds as it brings an aliveness expressed through our creativity.

Find a creative project or a class to allow those creative juices to flow. It is good for your whole body and brain, health, and wellbeing.

Honouring Your Body

The more spiritual focus you have—beginning with bringing the body back into balance by honouring it and meeting its needs—the more energy will flow back into your body. Honouring yourself, Nature, and the Life force that flows through all Life lifts your vibrations. You become more of a vibrational match for inspiration and Spirit to enter your consciousness and lift your awareness. The process is reciprocal. Honour your body; it honours you.

New Choices to Make

If we truly want to help heal our bodies and the Earth, we have to make different choices about how we live and how we think. Imagine health and disease at opposite ends of a continuum. Every choice moves us closer to one or the other.

Our world has become so toxic. Many governments have turned a blind eye to what has and is happening to compromise the health of the planet and, therefore, our own health. Every time we buy something, we are supporting the maker of that product or service.

Do we want to support the big corporations whose priority is profits for shareholders, not serving their customers? Or could we support local growers, manufacturers, and stores who follow ethical principles? It's our responsibility to do some research so we can make informed choices. What are we consenting to?

Frequency

Begin to think about what impacts you in terms of frequency. Everything has a vibrational frequency. Notice in your body how you respond to different things, such as certain people, places, food, music, and different movements, such as yoga, dancing, and walking. How you feel in your body will tell you if your current activity serves you or not.

Do you feel drained or energised, happy or sad or irritated? Cultivate these skills of knowing. Build your awareness. Learn to trust your gut and listen to your Heart's wisdom. What you learn will become your barometer for future choices.

Everything is energy. Match the frequency of the reality you want, and you cannot help but get that reality. It can be no other way.

—attributed to Albert Einstein

Everything vibrates from rocks to music, to thought, to the human body. The body is not just biological and chemical; it is electrical and can be measured. According to Dr. Kez Bridges, a healthy human body has a vibrational frequency range between 62–78 MHz. The higher the healthier! Higher frequencies hold more light. If our frequency drops below 62 MHz, the cells can start to change and mutate, the immune system becomes compromised, and illness manifests. If it drops to 58 MHz, cold and flu symptoms can appear, and at 55 MHz, candida is present. If the frequency drops to 52 or lower, Epstein-Barr virus (EBV) can result. Cancer can appear when the frequency drops to 42 MHz (Bridges 2023).

Remember we have the power to influence this by applying the practices shared so far to lift our vibes. It's all about the frequency. When the frequencies of our body interact with the frequencies in our environment, it can have a strengthening or weakening effect on our physical and mental wellbeing.

Additionally, a study of dental patients has shown that music played at 440 MHz generated more cortisol—and thus more anxiety—than music played at 432 MHz (Aravena 2020). Choose your frequencies with care.

Toxicity

One of the causes of disease is excessive toxicity. It can be defined as an introduction of an incompatible substance or frequency to the body system that is not able to be metabolised efficiently. This can lead to a buildup that produces a toxic environment, and the breakdown of the body begins. Wellness cannot be sustained long-term in such an environment.

Let's explore sources of toxicity to be aware of.

Agricultural Practices

Farming practices have changed dramatically in the last fifty years. The usage of chemicals has escalated—pesticides, including herbicides, fungicides, bactericides, insecticides, rodenticides, as well as synthetic fertilisers. According to Statista Research Department, in 2022, Brazil was the largest pesticide-consuming country in the world, consuming 800.65 thousand metric tons. The United States was second with 467.68 thousand metric tons (Statista Research Department 2024). That's just two countries! Globally, 3.69 million metric tons were spread in that year.

This must be impacting the health of the soil, food, and humans. These are artificial substances introduced to organic organisms, humans, and Nature. In many places after years of application, the soils are dying, so more chemicals, pesticides, and fertilisers are needed. These practices are unsustainable.

In March 2015, the International Agency for Research on Cancer (IARC), a specialised cancer agency of the World Health Organization (WHO), classified *glyphosate*, a key ingredient in most popular herbicide, Roundup, as "probably carcinogenic to humans." It also concluded that there was "strong evidence for genotoxicity" in experimental animals (IARC 2018).

Is this ingredient still being sold in products? Is the public informed about the risks?

Regenerative agriculture focuses on restoring ecosystems to improve soil health, water retention, and biodiversity to improve productivity and resilience. Fortunately, it is expanding around the world, a return to integrative, natural, sustainable practices. When implemented, this practice helps recover the health and fertility of the soil noticeably within a short time. Nature will respond when treated with respect.

Improving the health of soil could also improve the health and fertility of humans by reducing as much toxicity as possible. The change in this arena will come from the farmers themselves making a different choice. You could check out Farmer's Footprint (farmersfootprint.us) or Regen Farmer (regenfarmer.com) to see what is being done.

I suspect that GMO seeds and foods are not good for human and planetary health either. The fact that millions of dollars are spent in blocking proper labelling of the products made from GMO foods alarms me. Why does this process need to remain hidden? No long-term studies have been done that are publicly available. While most funded studies suggest that GMO foods are safe for consumption, others highlight potential risks that may warrant further investigation.

Guess who the guinea pigs are? A point to remember is that Nature or *natural* cannot be patented, so when a substance is altered, it can be patented, unique products can be created, and profits can be made.

Food Production

After crops have been produced and harvested, they go to manufacturers to make industrialised, processed products for consumption that we can buy in stores. This food is generally cheaper than fresh organic food, because many of the ingredients are subsidised by the government. Organic food, which has a higher frequency, is generally more expensive because growers have to pay for a licence to grow their produce without poisons. However, conventional growers using synthetic chemical products do not need a licence.

Why is that? Where is the logic? Who benefits? Who doesn't?

Water Pollution

Agricultural chemical runoff and industrial and mining pollutants find their way into watercourses, lakes, dams, oceans, and underground sources. This contamination affects the quality of water. Fluoride and chlorine or chloramine are the most common agents in water treatment. There has been controversy about both of them for decades.

Fluoride has had countless studies and meta-analysis studies that show it has potential to affect brain development in children, possibly leading to lower IQ. EPA officials have testified that fluoride is neurotoxic and could cause damage to the nervous system and brain (Borst 2024). It attracts calcium and can lead to calcification of the pineal gland, impacting the secretion of the hormone *melatonin* that regulates circadian rhythms, the sleep/wake cycle (Chlubek 2020).

In metaphysical circles, the pineal gland is a receiver and transmitter of information internally and externally. This gland supports tuning in to our intuition, creativity, and our divinity, our connection with Source.

Chlorine is a disinfectant that kills bacteria, viruses, and fungi. If it kills all bacteria, good or bad, how does it affect our microbiome, immune system, the manufacture of hormones in our gut, and, therefore, our brain health? Public health policy says that both of these are safe and effective to support human health.

Different opinions are seen as conspiracy theories (Unde 2018). Please do your own research and decide if investing in a water filter could be a good idea.

Air Pollution

Air pollution is mostly a consequence of industrial processes and aerosols sprayed into the air. Our biggest challenge in this area is geoengineering, sometimes called *chemtrails*. Contrails absolutely exist; they are the water vapour that disappears within seconds or minutes. The heavy white lines that drift, a.k.a. chemtrails, in the sky can last for hours and seem to fill our skies with a pale substance like dust or ash. They seem relentless and make it hard to see clear blue skies anymore. They have grown significantly paler since my childhood. I am not an expert in this area, but my gut tells me this is not good. I believe they contain contaminants that impact our health and that of our soils and water and are blocking the vital life-giver, our sun.

In May 2025, Florida banned geoengineering, the second state to do so after Tennessee. The UK has recently announced it will conduct experiments to reflect the sun. It does not sound like a clever idea to me, no matter how altruistic and logical it sounds. These are real-world experiments being conducted over real people without our informed consent (King 2025).

What is in those aerosols? Could it be harmful to human and planetary health? What are the consequences of blocking the sun, giver of life? Who benefits? Who does not?

Check the References and Resources at the end of the book to build awareness.

Electromagnetic Frequencies (EMF)

We have become an electrified society from all of our home lighting and appliances, street lighting, offices, neon signs, and a huge array of electronic devices, such as computers, phones, and cell towers. These waves can penetrate the tissues of the body (Kaszuba-Zwoinska 2015).

We are living in a soup of electromagnetic waves that is escalating rapidly, which may not support human health. In recent years, hundreds if not thousands of articles have been written and summits held about the deleterious effects of wireless technology and other aspects (Transformation Paradigm 2025). These summits explore how it is particularly harmful for children who are still developing their brains, nervous systems, and immune systems.

Personal Care Products

A guideline you could follow: If you can't put a substance in your mouth without poisoning yourself, why put it on your skin? All these extra chemicals end up in your liver to detoxify. If you can't pronounce it, research it: it is probably a chemical. Seek out products that are natural, plant-based, and organic if possible. Or make some yourself.

There are many online resources you could check out. If you wear makeup, find the most natural you can. Avoid anything with aluminum found in many deodorants. Avoid synthetic fragrances and cheap lathering agents. Learn to read labels.

Check the safety data sheets for each product that will at least show you the ingredients. Then, you can research those.

It's a lot of work. I did a lot over the years. Now I choose simple. I find the most natural products made by people and companies I trust to have ethical principles.

Home Care Products

There are so many products for cleaning. It can be confusing. Detoxifying your home supports your body, mind, and soul one step at a time. Keep it as simple as possible. Again, check labels. I rarely buy anything from a supermarket. Consider buying cleaning products that are plant-based from a health food shop or make your own. Pure essential oils can be amazing for so many things around the house—cleaning, healing, smelling good. They can replace germicides, insecticides, and other chemicals. Some chemicals can cause headaches or rashes and may be endocrine disrupters.

Plastics can mimic oestrogen, and we now have an overload in our bodies, even in newborns. Could this be one of the things that contribute to infertility issues?

Gardening Products

This problem is much the same as agricultural practices. Minimise chemicals and research natural ways of growing plants. If we want to be as healthy as possible—and the planet as well—we have to explore different ways of growing our gardens. Companion plants for growing different vegetables work well. For example, growing basil next to tomatoes. Basil's strong aroma helps control insects, and having different plants adds diversity to the garden. There are many suggestions online that gardeners have noted.

Clothing

If it is not made with natural fibres, such as cotton, wool, linen, or hemp, it is synthetic material. Many synthetics are made from petroleum-based polymers—a type of plastic—such as polyester, nylon, or acrylic. Skin is porous and can absorb some of these materials that have negative consequences over time. Skin needs to breathe, which natural fibres allow. Choose cotton underwear if possible. Also be aware that certain chemicals can be used in the growing and processing of the natural fibres. Find the least tainted. I can attest to organic cotton feeling heavenly.

Medications

Many over-the-counter and prescription drugs and other medicinal products are manufactured with petrochemicals, such as antibacterials, suppositories, cough syrups, lubricants, creams and gels, and others (CAPP 2025). If a condition is acute and life-threatening, perhaps conventional medicine is the best option. For chronic issues, consider exploring more natural options, such as plant-based products or herbs or a natural medicine practitioner.

Mainstream Media

Mainstream media is owned by the stakeholders of the narratives, and these outlets are paid to support the official narrative. Their coverage is usually filled with drama, negativity, and doom and gloom to generate fear that will lower your vibes. I'm not denying there are real situations, but if an event is not affecting you or loved ones personally, perhaps send your Light to these situations for the highest good while utilising positive, uplifting practices to maintain and increase your equilibrium. This is essential to maintain your power by mastering your energies to create good for your body, life, and the world.

Judgements and Guilt

My spiritual teacher said that judgement and guilt are major contributors to disharmony, leading to disease in your body. I definitely agree with that. Long-term stress chemicals in the body are a source of toxicity and have deleterious effects on your body that works hard to metabolise them. Work with the Tools of Consciousness to dissolve this negativity. This is a high priority for your health and wellbeing.

Disempowering Relationships

There may be people in your life that keep you in stress mode, obviously not good for your wellbeing. Avoid or reduce time with them if possible. Continue to do the inner work to master your emotions so these people will become less relevant. The more you care for yourself, the stronger and more resilient you become. You will be in a better position to make the best decisions to support yourself on your journey.

This information barely touches the tip of the iceberg about toxicity in our world. I do not mean to overwhelm or frighten you. Make the best, most informed choices you can, and over time, you may will get a different result. It's all growth, awareness, and taking different actions.

There are people all around the world gathering information in different areas and storing it safely, so when the time comes and the world is a safer place, it will be disclosed. At that time, interests vested in maintaining the status quo will be disarmed and no longer able to silence people.

If anything piques your curiosity, check out References and Resources.

CHAPTER 9

Harnessing Your Brilliant Mind and Emotions

Manifestation Through the Heart

Our mind and emotions are our major manifesting tools. We are all powerful creators. We have created our lives and this world so far, albeit mostly unconsciously. I wonder what else we could create with conscious intention in co-creation with the forces of Life. Ultimately, this is a partnership with Life, the Universe—a dance with the Divine.

Everything is frequency, and everything is connected. That is the nature of life. We live in an interconnected universe. You are a specific unique frequency. We all have our own unique energy signature.

Western culture has taught us to honour the servant, the mind, and to disregard and override the master, the Heart. Our emotions and intuition have been downgraded, subdued, ridiculed, and labelled irrational and, therefore, not worthy in a society that only values intelligence quotient (IQ). Emotional intelligence quotient (EQ) has been sorely missing in our culture, creating distorted systems. We need both for a healthy, functioning world.

Emotional intelligence is now being seen as a valued and necessary component to create a better, kinder world. I believe EQ is embodied by the sensitives, intuitives, creatives, the different thinkers, the deep feelers—all those who have been cast to the fringes of society in a world that did not accept them because they did not fit the standard model we were taught we had to fit into. We were told: *Be normal. Don't rock the boat. Fit in.* There is no normal in terms of personality, only uniqueness. Let our uniqueness be the new normal in our own lives.

Did you know that the heart has 5000 times more electromagnetic frequency than the brain? In 1991, it was discovered that the heart has 40,000 neurons, brain-like cells, that have capacity for sensing, thinking, feeling, and remembering independently from the brain (Morales 2020). I believe the Heart is the first organ to form as the embryo pulses itself into life after conception (EurostemCell 2024) and the last organ to shut down at the transition we call death (Morales 2020).

Clearly, our Heart is way more than a mechanism for pumping the blood around the body. It can see the bigger picture, make the connections, and help you align with your gifts and purpose once you establish a conscious relationship with this part of yourself. The Heart cannot lie. The mind can and does. It makes up all sorts of stories, reasons, and justifications based on your beliefs, perceptions, and interpretations to *keep you safe.* Growth is scary. Change is scary. These musings can limit you and keep you stuck.

We are moving into new territory in this world, and the mind may not be able to figure out what is going on or what to do because there isn't a precedent. In this case, you will need to follow your Heart. It will be your guiding Light as you navigate new territory.

This means the Heart has a greater capacity to rise above the manufactured and orchestrated separations the conditioned mind creates between people, such as culture, colour, religion, beliefs, politics, unequal opportunities, and more. The mind can deceive us much of the time because of the conditioning we've been steeped in our whole lives. All this conditioning enters the subconscious, which is like a lower mind out of our awareness. Then, that subconscious gets triggered in certain situations, and we make judgements and say and take actions from that unaware space.

The marriage between the Heart and the mind, the intuitive and the logical, the Feminine and Masculine principles within us and around us is so needed to raise our frequency, increase coherence, and heal ourselves and the world. Love is the highest frequency. It is the essence of the Creator, the source of all things.

The Difference Between Real and Imagined

However, do not discount the mind's capabilities as a brilliant strategist, planning how to get from A to B in tasks, such as building a house or following a map. It is also a crucial tool in manifesting because it has such rich imagination. However, it does *not* know the difference between real and imagined. That is why when you think about old traumas that happened in the past, you might retraumatise yourself, re-shock your nervous system as if it is happening now. Or if you imagine bad things happening in your future, it's like pre-traumatising yourself when it's not even happening and may not ever. Chronic judgement, guilt, and anger can suppress the immune system for hours, days, even years if we don't stop ourselves. The mind needs clear direction and clear boundaries. It is your responsibility to choose your focus.

Exercise

Begin to visualise what you do want to create in your life, not what you don't want. Then, enrich that positive vision with more colour, more brightness, more animation, and beautiful sounds of excitement or calm, always inviting.

What does your desire look like now? Describe it in detail.

What does it feel like when you imagine you already have it in your life?

Explore those feelings. Can you name them?

Take some time just to dream, imagine, check it out. Is it aligned with your values? Does it expand your heart? Does it allow you to develop and expand your talents? Does it bring more joy? Can you share the joy with others?

Journal about your insights.

That's the magic sauce, our emotions. Our emotions influence our reality. They hold a particular frequency that contributes to what we experience, personally and collectively. We want to choose the highest emotions we can. Someone else laughing can often lift our own spirits. Happiness influences everything else, including our relationships, food, pets, plants, and more. Experiments have been done with school children in which two identical plants are brought into the classroom. The first one is praised, told how beautiful it is, how much it is loved. The other is ignored or told it's ugly and other unkind things. That one withers, the first one blooms beautifully.

This experiment teaches us:

- Everything is interconnected.
- We can communicate with plants.
- Our thoughts and emotions affect reality.
- Choose the good emotions.
- Stay conscious as much as possible.

Change your thoughts and emotions when you notice your emotions dropping or anxiety rising. You have the power to do that. It's all about raising the frequency of our emotions that affect our wellbeing and ripple out to touch others.

Beliefs

Beliefs are not necessarily truths. They are usually based on someone else's reality, and you get to choose whether they are working for you or not. If not, you can choose something more empowering and aligned with your Truth. It may feel strange at first, but practice, play, ponder, and even pretend if that works for you. Check it out and see how it feels. This is how you stretch your comfort zone by doing something different.

You may even feel like an imposter. Much has been shared about *imposter syndrome,* but consider that the true imposter syndrome is when we are not being our True Self, when we are showing up as a diminished version of ourselves covered with labels and stories, acting out of a limited belief system. We do that to make others feel more comfortable, to make them accept us because we believe our uniqueness is not good enough, is too different. We fear we won't be able to belong or fit in.

If this is the case for you, maybe it's time to find a new tribe, new friends.

Beliefs are created through our culture, family dynamics, schools, religious institutions, figures of authority, media, friends, peer groups, and work colleagues—or any significant event or person that impacts you. They mostly exist just outside of conscious awareness and become visible when we are triggered and react to something someone said or did, and we suddenly find ourselves in a very uncomfortable place.

That's the time to catch the pattern: First, what is your belief about yourself? Then, what do you believe about the other person? The situation?

Ponder, get curious, get serious, drill down until you find what the underlying beliefs are. It may take several attempts. Be patient; be kind. It is often about unworthiness.

It's crucial to understand that the meaning you make of it, and what you think that says about you, others, and the world is what maintains that belief in your consciousness. This, in turn, informs your self-concept, who you believe yourself to be and the experiences you attract. Life responds to who you are being based on your beliefs about yourself, not who you are.

Your work ahead is to discover who you are not and let it all go. What reveals itself eventually is the true you, that which has always been present but has been covered over with erroneous beliefs, labels, and old stories about what happened in the past. This is the sacred work of letting go and revealing your True Self.

Most of us have a version of an unworthiness belief running in the background. You could begin the process of disentangling from that by committing to play with this new belief, inspired by my training with Dr Claire Zammit:

I am worthy purely because I exist.
My worth is not up for negotiation.
I am enough.
There is no need to prove my worthiness to anyone, including myself. Ever.
I am that already.

There may be some resistance that comes up with those statements, all sorts of arguments as to why you think they may not be true. That one is nonnegotiable. You are a unique creation of the Creator, and it does not make junk.

Exercise

Try saying the above words out loud. Notice any objections you may have to receiving this new awareness. Play with it.

Wonder: *Could this possibly be true?*

If it were indisputably true, how would that change your life?

How would you be feeling? What would that enable you to do?

What insights do you have?

Journal about what is being revealed to you.

Ask the questions and give yourself time to ponder possible responses. Extend patience and kindness to yourself as you practise new skills because change is not an overnight thing. Cultivating these skills like flowers in a garden can be an experience of beauty worth waiting for.

It's your responsibility to gently approach expanding your comfort zone to include your innate worthiness as the foundation. Growth can be uncomfortable, but change doesn't happen inside your comfort zone. The more you resist, the more uncomfortable it can become. Sometimes pressure is part of the process because you might just pop out of the place you thought was your comfort zone into new, uncharted territory.

Undoubtedly that will happen, and you can see it as scary or as an adventure. It is always your choice. Start with a bit of both if that feels safer. What if life truly could be an adventure, instead of something to be endured, depressed, or anxious about? What mindset shift could happen?

I think many may have a challenge loving ourselves because when we look inside, we see the labels and stories we have identified with and feel we can't love that person. We cannot see ourselves in the Truth because the limiting stories we believe about ourselves are in the way. Our work is to witness, hold, forgive, release, and integrate back into our wholeness.

I believe we are all good, caring beings at our core, wanting to love and be loved. If we are not expressing that, we are operating under faulty belief systems about ourselves and the world that we have allowed to be installed in our consciousness. Remember, beliefs are not necessarily Truths. Utilise those beliefs that serve your greatest happiness and health, and let the others go.

Conditioning

There is no *normal* in terms of personality. We all have unique personalities and expressions. Normal is an artificial construct and fictitious belief perpetuated by a system that demands conformity to its rules for its own ends. Conformity starts early. We tend to take on our parents' beliefs about themselves and life, what is acceptable or not.

As children, we attended school in uniforms, sitting in rows, not allowed to interact, offer different ideas, daydream, or access our imaginations, repeating ad infinitum what we were told to think, believe, and do, so we could be useful in the system that might employ us later. If we repeated enough of the *normal* and correct narratives, beliefs, and behaviours, we were told we would be rewarded, more readily accepted, and employed and, therefore, perpetuate the system.

If we didn't obey, we risked being ostracised. The fear of not belonging is huge and leads to self-criticism and shutting down of parts of the Self.

As young adults, we were shown via media and societal narratives that to be accepted we must think a certain way, look a certain way—wear these clothes, this makeup, that perfume—drive certain cars, drink certain drinks, eat these foods, speak a certain way. These behaviours and beliefs became normalised and continued. Somewhere in there, the real us—the unique person we each are—grew confused, covered up, lost, and quieted for a long time.

Then, the cracks start to appear. Maybe we feel as if we are going crazy. It can be frightening. What if these symptoms are messages calling from our True Self for authentic expression, not that of the herd? Those longings and yearnings and whispers of the Soul we have spent years avoiding want a voice.

Perhaps we no longer want to play the game of normal, bland, predictable lives. Perhaps we don't want the old story of success being about studying hard, getting a good job, climbing the ladder, and earning big bucks. Maybe there is a different choice we can make. Maybe exploring who we are, developing our potential in different ways, is what makes our Heart sing. That's worth going after, even if it may mean going against all our conditioning, social acceptance, and society's expectations. That can be very liberating.

> *Oh God, help me believe the truth about myself, no matter how beautiful it is.*
>
> —Macrina Wiederkehr, Benedictine Nun

Trauma

Three levels of trauma have been identified by Thomas Hübl—individual, ancestral, and collective (Hübl 2023). We generally experience all three to varying degrees, which can make life more challenging, but not insurmountable. I am no trauma expert, but what I know to be true is that Love and compassion heal. One of the beautiful things about the massive wave of the awakening of humanity is the growing awareness of trauma. Much research has been done and continues to more deeply understand it. We are realising that it affects all of us. Gabor Mate, MD, has written many brilliant books that could help.

Individual Trauma

Everyone has gone through some form of trauma, and this looks different for each individual. For many of us, bad things happened when we were younger, and we didn't have the understanding nor capacity to deal with it, so we offloaded it into our subconscious, into our body, out of our awareness so we could survive childhood and adolescence and function in life as a grown-up. For most of us, that was our best choice at the time. It was a normal response to an abnormal situation. That needs to be acknowledged.

However, trauma left unresolved will impact your ability to create what you want in life, including your health, aligned relationships, and work that you enjoy. Some research suggests that there is a link between past trauma and chronic disease (NWC 2020). Unresolved trauma creates stories that we continue to tell ourselves about ourselves, others, and life.

Healing from trauma is deep work, and you may need assistance to do this safely. There is no shame in this. If you feel you need help, find trained, trauma-informed people or a group where you can support each other in the healing journey (see Resources). You can begin the process by having self-compassion and understanding because you've been through a lot.

It's no wonder you feel this way. However, hard as it was, tough as it was, something in you allowed your life to continue. Perhaps there was a reason for that trauma and that your life continued. Just be open to any deeper learnings, whatever they could be. Let your curiosity open the door for new awareness of possibilities that perhaps you could not see before. Part of what we are here to learn is to love unconditionally, starting with the Self. It's a journey and a destination.

Sometimes it is hard to change, to grow, to heal, when you don't know what's ahead. When the something you yearn for is outside of your lived experience, it may seem impossible. Old beliefs and traumas continue to be triggered and inform actions to help keep you *safe*. However, the *safe* of where you are eventually becomes more uncomfortable than the fear of changing and moving into the unknown. When this happens, the desire for change can move you to act.

The unknown and the uncertain could be where your liberation lies.

Ancestral Trauma

There have been some studies recently by people looking at generational and ancestral trauma on mice and rats. They suggest that severe trauma experienced by one generation produced certain responses, and that multiple generations down the line still produced the same response to the same stimuli, even though they had never experienced it themselves or had living contact with those who had (Nuwer 2013). Some of what we experience may come from our mothers, fathers, grandmothers, and grandfathers and beyond. The beautiful thing is that when you begin to heal, you are healing trauma for generations to come and the generations that have been. That is powerful.

Collective Trauma

The deep work ahead for all of us is to heal from the trauma our broken dysfunctional systems have perpetrated upon us. As an example, the last five years have traumatised everyone, and if there was trauma in your life beforehand, it is likely to have been compounded. When people are living in trauma and have no way of resolving it, life can become difficult and disturbing and could result in erratic behaviours and an inability to think clearly.

Trauma revs up our nervous systems to the point of exhaustion and reduces our cognitive ability by shutting down that part of the brain that solves problems. Learning new things can become much harder, resilience wanes, and hope can seem like a distant dream. When the collective is traumatised, it creates systems that perpetuate more trauma (Hübl 2023).

Exercises to Heal from Trauma

1. This is your sacred work, coming home to yourself, touching all the places that hurt with your love. Many sensitive people try to numb themselves, to block out the pain. They can also feel other people's pain and often can't distinguish what is theirs and what is not. Their receptors for pain and injustice are wide open, and they feel it deeply.

If all you can do in the moment is ask the question: *Who does this belong to?* it might give you some relief.

I still use this question if I notice my energy has dropped, and I'm not feeling okay. I know the feeling is built on a story that my subconscious is rolling out as another opportunity to witness, to feel, to reassure myself that I am still whole.

The feeling will dissipate if it's not yours. If it stays, it's yours to resolve. Just acknowledge that you feel it and address it when you can.

Prepare the space, light a candle, be out in Nature, say a prayer, call in the highest Light, or whatever will bring you comfort and calm.

First, you need to be able to source from the functional, more powerful part of yourself that helps others freely in their time of need. Now, turn that part towards yourself before welcoming in the traumatised part of yourself. Think about where you feel most like yourself, where you feel strong and able to access your resources and be resilient, and imagine stepping into that space. Embody that space and the feeling. If you are steeped in the feelings of the trauma, you are not at your most powerful.

You need to create safety within and around you. Take time, breathe in slowly and deeply, place your hand on your Heart to awaken it to your intent. Think about or visualise something you love that makes you happy, something you're grateful for in your life. Make sure you take the time to feel those positive feelings in your body. This brings Heart and brain into coherence, enabling you to come into relationship with the upset feelings with more safety (Duqum 2024).

2. When you are ready, you can place one hand on your Heart and the other on your belly. Take a breath and release slowly. Visualise or imagine yourself as your caring adult self being with that younger aspect of you that got trapped in a story. Be willing to go deep to sit with the aspect of yourself that holds those upset feelings attached to the story. Remember they are a normal response to an abnormal situation. Witness them and come into greater acceptance. Things happened and you had no control.

3. Create a little distance from the actual feelings by staying in your adult self so they don't overwhelm you. Can you name them? Is it fear, grief, sadness, anger, distress, hate, or something else? When we name the feelings, it puts a Light on them, so they recognise they have been seen and acknowledged. It can bring relief. These aspects

> and feelings need your kindness, compassion, and care to begin the healing. Let your younger self know it is loved, and your intention is to heal and reintegrate that part into wholeness. You are doing the best you know how. If the tears come, let them flow. They help the healing process.

Trauma acknowledged is trauma that can be healed. It may take a few attempts. Always keep yourself safe. If it feels unsafe, withdraw. Breathe. Give yourself a big hug and tell yourself how brave and amazing you are. Well done.

People Are Mirrors

You can't see in someone else what you don't have. You will have no reference point for that quality. People are our mirrors. That's the bad news and the good news. If you are judging someone else, you will need to ask yourself where that same characteristic is inside you. How does that play out?

It may not be obvious—usually it's not—but somewhere you will see where you are being dishonest with yourself or others in whatever you are judging them for. Maybe it's bullying yourself or others. Continue to observe. Conversely, if you see someone's brilliance, you may ask where you are brilliant in your own unique way and how you can use that for yourself and others.

Patterns in Your Life

We all have them. If you find repeating patterns in your life—in relationships, health, or finances—they are here to teach you something about yourself. Through these patterns, you can see your growth edges and learn from them. Accept and understand where they may have originated so you can heal the patterns and create happier more aligned beliefs, behaviours, and circumstances. When you become conscious of those patterns and name them, you can use the tools to release them.

The patterns that began to reveal themselves through my challenges were the ubiquitous ones of unworthiness, not good enough, seeking approval from others, being a people pleaser. I have come to realise that if I am still breathing, there is likely more to do—not as a chore, not with a sinking feeling, but with gratitude for the journey, the learnings, and the opportunity to spiral higher.

If you want to awaken all of humanity, then awaken all of yourself. If you want to eliminate the suffering in the world, then eliminate all that is dark and negative in yourself. Truly the greatest gift you have to give is that of your own self-transformation.
—Lao Tzu, Chinese Philosopher, Founder of Taoism

CHAPTER 10

Creating a Vision for Your Life

Up to this point, you have been on an epic journey learning more about the backdrop to how and why the world is as it is, and why things need to be done differently. You have been working through the exercises and discovering more about yourself.

- You have been learning to sit in wonder and curiosity to be open to new possibilities, to ask the questions to open the space as opposed to looking for the one solution.
- You have been practicing being kinder to yourself, bringing in compassion for the steep learning curve in your journey of life so far.
- You are creating a relationship with your body, communicating with it and learning to serve its needs.
- You are feeling more connected to your feelings, honouring them, nurturing yourself, and practicing noticing the felt sense of a yes and a no in your body.
- You are learning to monitor your thoughts and to

direct your mind into positive creations you want to participate in.
- You may be feeling into the possibilities for developing your potential in ways you haven't considered before, ways that inspire and excite you.

Here are some questions for you to ponder to gain greater clarity about what you want your life to be, to create a vision that will magnetise it to you. Take your time, one a day or more, and journal after each question to help you work out where you are and where you want to be:

- What are the qualities you want to experience in life, such as joy, happiness, fulfillment?
- What area of your life do you want to transform, such as career, health, relationships, finances? If more than one, choose the one that energises you most.
- What is it you deeply yearn for in your life? What holds the most energy for you?
- What do you think has stopped you up until now? Is that belief true? You may need to identify and break through some of the old limiting stories. What are your beliefs about yourself in this area? What are your beliefs about others and how the world might receive this new version of you?
- What old stories and beliefs still deplete you and need your healing, love, and compassion?

Use the Tools of Consciousness to gain greater clarity and resolution. Play with creating new beliefs that serve you and your higher purpose. Even if it feels like you're making it up, create a new story starting with, *I am now living the life of my dreams* and name what that means to you and what you will feel as though you are already there. That last part is really important. Act as if you already have what you desire and feel the delicious fulfilment of that.

The power of aligning your thoughts, which are electrical energy, and your feelings, which are magnetic energy, is exponential. It's more than just thoughts and affirmations. Feelings are the juice that facilitates the manifestation of thoughts through your actions towards that dream.

Now, move on to the following questions:

- Where do you feel the most powerful, the most like you, the most alive, the most aligned on-purpose?
- What do you love to do that makes you light up?
- What can you do easily that other people find hard?
- What type of people do you like to hang out with?
- What type of people would you like to serve? What age group are they?
- If there were no perceived obstacles, what could be possible for you?

The answers will give you a better idea of where and how you might like to serve others, perhaps creating new work for yourself.

When you create a new story of your choice, you begin to create different neural pathways in your brain that lead to a new self-identity.

Create a vision statement starting with:

*I am now creating*_______________________________.
*I am now living*_______________________________.
*I am now experiencing*_______________________________.
*I am now expressing*_______________________________.

Fill in the blanks with whatever you can see and feel in your future. Play with them; be bold, even if it feels like a pretend game. That's where it starts—in your imagination. There's a reason you chose what you are now imagining, because that is yours to do. It won't be the same in other people's imagination. Yours will be unique because you are unique.

*You are never given a dream without also being given
the power to make it come true. You may have to work
for it, however.*
—Richard Bach, *Illusions: The Adventures of a
Reluctant Messiah*

Moving forward, you may want to create intentions around your vision on what you intend in your life, how you want to live it, experience it, and express it. Let the Universe know what you want to manifest into your reality. Visualise it; feel it like a new melody in your body.

Next, answer the following questions:

- What is one small doable but stretching action step you can take in that direction?
- What is a reasonable time frame for that to happen?

- What support might you need?
- Who can you seek support from?
- Do you need to learn new skills? Where can you do that?
- What insights have you gained from this process?

You are creating a destiny pathway, which means you must stay open, receptive, and curious. Stay tuned in to your intuition, listen and watch for clues, and follow the sparkly breadcrumbs. Notice the excitement in your body when you think about something you want to do, express, experience, or contribute. The excitement is generated by your Heart and will guide and support you on your next steps towards manifesting your vision, your dream. You have to have a dream for that dream to come true.

Reflections

One of the central learnings here is to realise you always have a choice. You can make decisions that enhance your life—or not. You can always choose your responses to things that are not in your control. When I left home, that was my turning point to realise I had co-created the situation with my husband by choices I made to please others at the expense of myself. I could, therefore, make different choices to re-create a very different scenario. That choice is where the power lies.

We have a choice in how we create our personal lives, and globally, humanity has a choice in the way we want to live with Mother Earth. We have all contributed to major imbalances and dysfunction by our unconscious agreements, choices, and behaviours. We can create differently by making informed conscious choices about how we want to live, claiming our sovereignty, and then making decisions that support us all as we build a new reality. We move from a constructed, fear-based reality to one based on kindness, cooperation, and sustainability that is more community based.

In these transitional times from the old to the new, we need to be resourceful and resilient. By healing and balancing ourselves physically, emotionally, and mentally as much as possible, we are building a new foundation and will be more resourceful for the changes ahead. We are in the greatest paradigm shift for thousands of years. It could get rough.

Our personal choices create our inner and outer worlds. One person at a time making wiser choices creates a bigger, faster effect until all of humanity and our planet are brought into greater healing and eventual thriving, our natural birthright. It changes the whole game.

I have often thought that life is a game of "Pin the Tail on the Donkey," wearing a blindfold, stabbing in the dark, listening to the feedback from the outer world. We now need to turn inwards, into our bodies and our Hearts and listen to inner feedback with curiosity and without judgement:

- What are we thinking?
- What are we eating or drinking?
- What are we speaking?
- Who are we spending time with?
- How does each choice make us feel? Good or not so good?
- Are we on track?

Perhaps we need to course-correct, making different, wiser, life-enhancing choices.

There is no wrongness or badness here, simply learning situations. That's how life serves us in presenting different scenarios for us to learn from, to know what serves us and our health and wellbeing. And what doesn't. You will absolutely know when you arrive at the right place. You will feel it in your whole body. That's your inner knowing. You do not need anyone else's validation to know that.

Writing this book, I often thought about a movie called *The NeverEnding Story* (1984). It's a kids' adventure movie of challenges and possibilities to conquer fears and doubts. It has magic, tough times, dark forces, a freedom warrior, a princess, a luck dragon, and the triumph of coming through all the challenges.

The story is about a little boy, Sebastian, who finds an old book and begins to read it, and he finds himself in The Story—being in the book and reading the book. Near the end of the story, the little girl, a princess of another world where dark forces are destroying her planet, asks Sebastian to give the planet a new name, a new vibration so it can be saved and regenerated.

It's the name. It's the voice. It's the sound. It's the frequency.

This movie was so deep and meaningful for me. Sebastian doesn't believe that he's the one who can make a difference. In the end, the forces of darkness are whipping up a storm around him, and he's still doubting. He finally goes to the window, pushes it open, and calls out the name of his much-loved mother. We don't hear the name as the storm is so fierce. Then everything calms down and is quiet and peaceful. Life begins anew.

Sebastian played his part. He answered the calling even though he doubted, afraid and uncertain. He stepped forward, and, in doing so, he changed his belief about himself to effect change in the world. By taking action, he changed his self-identity and was able to help change everything.

I so related to this movie, even though I could not draw the parallels at the time—of writing a book, being in the book, and experiencing the doubt that I had a part to play in the trajectory of where humanity seemed to be going.

Are you feeling you have a part to play? Are you doubting yourself and your abilities to create change? Taking an action step in the direction of your dreams, no matter how small, can change everything.

Play with: What name or vibration would you choose for your world? I pondered for a moment, and the word *love* popped in. Then I remembered that *earth* becomes *heart* if we move the last letter to the front. I found that significant, hiding in plain sight as many Truths are. Is it a sign?

Many of us as sensitives, empaths, dreamers, heart-centred leaders, and visionaries who are destined to be the changemakers have made ourselves wrong, less than, or too different. Therefore, we may have deduced that we must hide our differences, our uniqueness. Otherwise, we fear we won't be accepted; we won't belong.

Let us consider that we belong to ourselves first as free beings, and that we must become our own best friends. Self-supporting not self-sabotaging. Then, we will attract those of like mind and like-heartedness.

I judged and criticised myself for my different ways of seeing, thinking, being, and believing. It seemed deficient, messy, illogical. *Oh, thank goodness!* is all I can say now.

There is great need for different perspectives in this world. The continuation of similar thinking has led to many of our problems, and we cannot solve them from the level of thinking that created them. The world needs different thinkers with different perspectives to contribute to the healing and flourishing of humanity to return to its majestic, benevolent, true nature.

Are you the one the world has been waiting for?

Celebrating Life

The real secret to a fabulous life is to live imperfectly with great delight.

—Leigh Standley Sherri

You have experienced a lot of challenges in your life, and you have or are overcoming them one by one, because as a conscious, caring, aware person, you are practicing to become a responsible co-creator, making wise choices that serve you, others, and the planet. If something comes up in your field that feels out of alignment with who you are becoming, welcome it as an opportunity to rise higher, to learn what is going on in your own consciousness.

Ask what story or issue has surfaced for you to witness, acknowledge, be curious about, embrace, heal, love, resolve, and integrate back into wholeness. And each time you become clearer, more energised, happier, more peaceful, and more aligned, you circle higher in your consciousness.

I am celebrating you—your courage and resilience, your willingness to learn, grow, and evolve your consciousness, to be prepared to make different choices, to heal old stories, to be curious about what's opening up for you and exploring what else may be possible. You are practicing to be compassionate, kind, and patient with yourself. You have accepted the challenges of life and are doing your best to navigate and steer yourself towards safety and empowerment. I salute you and your beautiful, intelligent, passionate Heart that has brought you to this point.

I recently celebrated a significant birthday with a group of longtime friends at a local winery that has beautiful food and organic wine and lovely, happy staff. I usually celebrate birthdays with family at home, and I cook, so it was an absolute treat to share this occasion with people who accept and love me. What a gift that is.

I know I am blessed to have had this experience, especially when the whole restaurant of 100 people erupted into a joyous version of the "Happy Birthday" song. This event was organised by my husband while I was outside for a few minutes, looking at the beautiful garden. That act healed a lot of old hurts as I felt seen, heard, and honoured.

There were other people celebrating birthdays too. The vibe affected everyone there: strangers were hugging each other, and the staff were all beaming appreciation for the moment. This is what life is about—sharing the simple pleasures of connection and celebration of life, in small ways or big.

I live in gratitude for each day, and I feel the presence of grace in my life. That attitude attracts more good things into my life. It's a beautiful cycle.

Where you can, give thanks, appreciate yourself and others and the world around you that has taught you much about who you have been showing up as, who you are becoming, what you are no longer willing to tolerate, and what you might contribute—big or small—to create the more beautiful world we all know is possible.

How can you bring your special brand of medicine to the world?

So here we sit, you and I in this field of connection, connected through our Hearts, and I ponder what is next for you and for me. I wonder what it would be like in the future as I reach my transition to the next level of life, to look back on my life and ask:

- Did I do what I came here to do?
- Did I fulfill my mission?
- Did I show up as my full self?
- Did I stand in my Light?
- Did I speak my Truth?
- Did I draw my line in the sand?
- Did I stand my ground?
- Did I make my voice matter and share my message?
- Was I grateful for all the hard horrible experiences I endured to gain the wisdom to heal, to know myself, and to love myself?
- Was I grateful for all the magnificence and beauty my Life held?

My body's response to these questions created a feeling like a gathering of the forces to celebrate, mobilise, embrace, enthuse, and create opportunities for my next step—whatever it may be and wherever it may lead. I invite you to ask these questions of yourself, to be open, curious, and wonder what else might be possible for you, your life, and this planet.

And, of course, to journal about any insights you have. Then re-read your journal to witness how far you have come on your beautiful homecoming journey to yourself.

May the *Divine Bless You* for the wondrous being you are and the sacred work you have done and are here to do. I honour you and salute the beautiful Soul that you are.

Love is always the answer. Welcome home.

AN INVITATION

If what you read in *The Turning Point for Humanity*
has been of value to you, please post a review at your
favourite online retailer. This will help me reach more
people with this message.

If you learned more about yourself and the world that you
can use for your highest good, please pass on the book
to someone else who may also benefit. Start a discussion
group; donate to a library or a women's shelter. Keep the
momentum going.

You are welcome to check out
theturningpointforhumanity.com
for more information and contact details.

Eternal gratitude,

Elizabeth Grace

ACKNOWLEDGMENTS

First and foremost, I'd like to thank my family for their encouragement, love, support, and patience.

To my daughter, whose unwavering support and love and enthusiasm kept me going even when I doubted myself. You carried the vision for me to head towards.

To my son and husband, thank you for all the love, support, and encouragement, and for the fodder to crack me open and embody my True Self.

To John-Roger, DSS, my Spiritual Teacher, Founder of the Movement of Spiritual Inner Awareness (MSIA), whose teachings brought the wisdom of the ages to my life that changed everything. A gift of practical spirituality, simplicity, common sense, and profound timeless wisdom and truths in a world that was clearly lacking those qualities. I am forever grateful.

To John Morton, DSS, Spiritual Director of MSIA, and successor to John-Roger, for holding the space for these teachings to expand into the world and for bringing even more Blessings to us all.

To Don Tolman who was the first person to introduce me to the powerful simple Principles of Health that he learned on his journey around the world to find the truth about long-lasting health and happiness. He has been called the Cowboy of Wholefoods Medicine. Thanks Don, for staying the course and educating so many of us.

To Dr. Claire Zammit, Founder of The Institute for Women-Centred Coaching and creator of Feminine Power trainings in coaching, facilitation, and leadership. Thank you for your brilliance in speaking to the hearts and minds of hundreds of thousands of women around the world seeking to make a difference.

To all my friends who supported me and knew when not to ask: *How's the book going*? Extra special thanks to Cindy and Liisa, my leadership group friends, who went above and beyond to encourage, prop me up when needed, and support me in every way possible. Especially Cindy who helped me with so many technological challenges. So much love and gratitude to you both. To the rest of the leadership girls for their belief in me and encouragement of my project and journey, I send much gratitude.

To Aedamar, my Soul Writing Coach, who began me on the journey of writing, whose profound meditations drew out of me the threads of this book. She encouraged me to put in personal stories to help make the book more relatable and powerful. Her keen insights have contributed greatly to bringing this book forward.

Last but definitely not least, eternal thanks to Seshat Publishing for their patience, support, kindness, encouragement, and belief that my book was worthy of publishing. To the editing team and other departments who had input, you did a brilliant job of midwifing this book into existence. Deep bow to all of you. I am so grateful for the journey and all the learnings gained.

REFERENCES

Arevena, Pedro Christian, Calmila Almonacid, and Marcelo Ignacio Mancilla. 2020. Effect of music at 432 Hz and 440 Hz on dental anxiety and salivary cortisol levels in patients undergoing tooth extraction: a randomized clinical trial." *Journal of Applied Oral Science.* 11 May. doi:_10.1590/1678-7757-2019-0601

Atkinson, Judy and Carly Atkinson. 2021 *Participants' Workbook: a study program for Healing People, Sharing Culture, Regenerating Communities: Trauma Informed Care and Practice—An Indigenous Approach to Developing Worker Skills.* We Al-li Pty Ltd.

Bernays, Edward. *Propaganda.* 1928. https://www.docdroid.net/ulvqryK/bernays-propaganda-pdf

Borst, Ellie and Miranda Willson. 2024. "EPA 'in a really tough spot' after landmark fluoride ruling." *E&ENews/Politico.* 18 October. https://www.eenews.net/articles/epa-in-a-really-tough-spot-after-landmark-fluoride-ruling/#:~:text=A%20long%20history&text=Experts%20generally%20agree%2C%20and%20EPA,public%20health%20pose%20health%20threats

Braden, Gregg. 2017. *The Science of Self-Empowerment: Awakening the New Human Story.* Hay House, Australia.

Braden, Gregg. 2020. "This Was Happening Long Before Humans Appeared on Earth." *Gregg Braden Official.* Nov 29. https://www.youtube.com/watch?v=CmSxaoXvYtl

Bridgeford, Ross. 2024. *The Alkaline Life: New Science to Rebalance Your Body, Reverse Ageing and Prevent Disease.* Hay House UK.

Bridges, Kez. 2023. "Raising Vibrational Frequency Naturally." *DrKezChirolab.* 19 April. https://drkezchirolab.com/blogs/news/raising-vibrational-frequency-naturally

Buckmiller Fuller Institute (BFI). 2024. "Systems Change." *Buckminster Fuller Institute.* https://www.bfi.org/about-fuller/big-ideas/systems-change/

Canadian Association of Petroleum Producers (CAPP). 2025. "Petroleum in Real Life." *Capp.* 31 May. https://www.capp.ca/en/oil-natural-gas-you/petroleum-and-real-life/

Chlubek, Dariusz and Maciej Sikora. 2020. "Fluoride and Pineal Gland." *Multidisciplinary Digital Publishing Institute: applied sciences.* 22 April. https://doi.org/10.3390/app10082885

Daniel, Pete. 2005. *Toxic Drift: Pesticides and Health Post-World War II South.* Louisiana State University Press. https://www.environmentandsociety.org/mml/toxic-drift-pesticides-and-health-post-world-war-ii-south

Dev Misra, Bibhu. 2023. *Yuga Shift: The End of the Kali Yuga & The Impending Planetary Transformation.* White Falcon Publishing.

Dillbeck, M. C. Landrith, G. and Orme-Johnson, D. W. 1981. "Transcendental Meditation Program and Crime Rate Change in a Sample of Forty-Eight Cities." *Journal of Criminal Justice.* Volume 4. https://www.ojp.gov/ncjrs/virtual-library/abstracts/transcendental-meditation-program-and-crime-rate-change-sample

Duqum, Andre. 2024. "3 POWERFUL Steps to Awaken HEART & Brain Connection (and the SCIENCE of it): Interview with Gregg Braden." *Know Thyself.* 26 April. https://www.youtube.com/watch?v=Tak9vZJ66mg

Emoto, Masaru. 2001. *The Hidden Messages in Water.* David A. Thayne, trans. Atria Books.

EuroStemCell. 2024. "The heart: our first organ." *EuroStemCell.* 06 October. https://www.eurostemcell.org/heart-our-first-organ

Gamble, Foster. 2018. "Let's Talk for Real About Humans and Climate Change." *Free to Thrive.* 14 September. https://www.freetothrive. com/blog/lets-talk-for-real-about-humans-and-climate-change/

Griffin, G. Edward. 1991. *The Creature from Jekyll Island: A Second Look at the Federal Reserve.* American Media.

Grewal, Harpal Singh. 2022. "How Leftover Bombs From World War 2 Became 'Fertilisers' for Agricultural Use." *Pure & Eco India.* 01 February. https://pureecoindia.in/how-leftover-bombs-from-world-war-2-became-fertilisers-for-agricultural-use/

Gustafson, Craig. 2017. "Bruce Lipton, PhD: The Jump From Cell Culture to Consciousness." *Integrative Medicine: A Clinician's Journal.* Dec, 44–50. https://www.ncbi.nlm.nih.gov/pmc/articles/PMC6438088/

Heer, Dain. 2024. "Who does this belong to?" *Dr. Dain Heer: Access Consciousness.* https://drdainheer.com/whodoesthisbelongto/

Hübl, Thomas. 2023. "Healing the Traumas That Shape Society." 30 November. https://thomashuebl.com/healing-the-traumas-that-shape-society/

International Agency for Research on Cancer (IARC). 2018. "IARC Monograph on Glyphosate." *IARC.* 19 July. https://www.iarc.who.int/ featured-news/media-centre-iarc-news-glyphosate/#:~:text=In%20 March%202015%2C%20IARC%20classified,of%20 %E2%80%9Cpure%E2%80%9D%20glyphosate

Ji, Sayer. 2025. "The Most Hormonally Regenerative Fruit on Earth." *GreenMedInfo.* 14 May. https://greenmedinfo.com/content/most-hormonally-regenerative-fruit-earth

Kaszuba-Zwoinska, Jerzy Gremba, Barbara Galdzinska-Calaik, Karolina Wojcik-Piotrowicz, and Thor Piotr. 2015. "Electromagnetic field induced biological effects in humans." *Przegl Lek. National Library of Medicine.* https://pubmed.ncbi.nlm.nih.gov/27012122/

King, Simon. 2025. "UK experiments to reflect sunlight one step closer." *BBC.* 07 May. https://www.bbc.com/weather/articles/c5ygydeqq08o

Land, George and Beth Jarman. 1992. *Breakpoint and Beyond: Mastering the Future Today.* Harper Business.

Lebow, Hilary. 2021. "Are You Absorbing Other People's Emotions?" *Psych Central.* 20 August. https://psychcentral.com/blog/stop-absorbing-other-peoples-emotions

Leister, Mitchell B. 2025. "The Medical Monopoly on Mental Health and the Flexner Report." *Psychology Today.* 24 February. https://www.psychologytoday.com/au/blog/the-leading-edge/202502/the-medical-monopoly-on-mental-health-and-the-flexner-report

Lipton, Bruce. 2005. *The Biology of Belief: Unleashing the Power of Consciousness, Matter, and Miracles.* Hay House.

Morales, Jessica. 2020. "The Heart's Electromagnetic Field Is Your Superpower: Training heart-brain coherence." *Psychology Today.* 29 November. https://www.psychologytoday.com/us/blog/building-the-habit-of-hero/202011/the-hearts-electromagnetic-field-is-your-superpower?msockid=29bf2d00f21c69960bb63911f32e6830

National Workforce Centre for Child Mental Health (NWC). 2020. "Adverse Childhood Experiences (ACEs): Summary of evidence and impacts." *Emerging Minds.* January. https://d2p3kdr0nr4o3z.cloudfront.net/content/uploads/2020/02/19102540/ACES-Summary-of-Evidence-and-Impacts-V2.pdf

Nuwer, Rachel. 2013. "Baby Mice Can Inherit Fear of Certain Smells From Their Parents." *Smithsonian Magazine.* 03 December. https://www.smithsonianmag.com/smart-news/baby-mice-can-inherit-fear-of-certain-smells-from-their-parents-180948096/

Petersen, Wolfgang, director. 1984. The NeverEnding Story. Warner Brothers.

Roth, Bob. 2012. "Maharishi on 'The 1% Effect'—How Just a Small Percentage of People Can Change the World." *Transcendental Meditation.* 11 May. https://usa.tm.org/blog/maharishi/maharishi-on-the-1-effect/

Porter, Eleanor H. 1913. *Pollyanna.* L. C. Page.

Saplakogu, Yasemin. 2023. "Is It Real or Imagined? Here's How Your Brain Tells the Difference." *Wired.* 27 August. https://www.wired.com/story/is-it-real-or-imagined-heres-how-your-brain-tells-the-difference/#:~:text=%E2%80%9CI%20can%20look%20outside%20my,Explained%20From%20Head%20to%20Toe

Schmoe, Jeremy. 2020. "Neuroscience Reveals: Gratitude Literally Rewires Your Brain." *The Functional Neurology Centre.* 10 October. https://thefnc.com/research/neuroscience-reveals-gratitude-literally-rewires-your-brain/

Shayne, Tasha. 2020. "Your Body Is a Superorganism Thanks to These Microbes." *Gaia.* 16 December. https://www.gaia.com/article/your-body-is-a-superorganism-thanks-to-these-microbes

Stastista Research Department. "Leading countries in agricultural consumption of pesticides worldwide in 2022." *Stastista.* 23 September. https://www.statista.com/statistics/1263069/global-pesticide-use-by-country/

82 Minerals. 2025. "Mineral Rich: The Secret Behind Authentic 82 Minerals Sea Salt." *82 Minerals—home page.* https://www.82minerals.com

Transformation Paradigm. 2025. "Transformation Into the New Paradigm." *Transformation Paradigm—home page.* https://transformationparadigm.com/new-technology/the-5g-crisis.html

Tucker, Mike. 2025. "Subconscious Mind Vs. Conscious Mind: What Is the Difference?" *Altered Mind Waves.* 27 May. https://alteredmindwaves.com/subconscious-mind-vs-conscious-mind-whats-the-difference/#:~:text=Your%20conscious%20mind%

Unde, Maitreyee, Raju Patil, and Peris Dastoor. 2018. "The Untold Story of Fluoridation: Revisiting the Changing Perspectives." *Indian Journal of Occupational & Environmental Medicine.* Sep–Dec, 121–127. doi:10.4103/ijoem.IJOEM_124_18

Urbano, Ana M. 2021. "Otto Warburg: The journey towards the seminal discovery of tumor cell bioenergetic reprogramming." *Biochimica et Biophysica Acta (BBA)—Molecular Basis of Disease. Volume 1867, Issue 1,* 01 January. https://doi.org/10.1016/j.bbadis.2020.165965

Weir, Peter, director. 1998. *The Truman Show.* Paramount Pictures.

Wigington, Dane. 2017. "Climate Engineering Fact And Photo Summary." *Geoengineering Watch.* 02 August. https://www.geoengineeringwatch.org/climate-engineering-fact-and-photo-summary/

Wigington, Dane. 2018. "Exposing the Climate Engineering Cover-Up: Geoengineering Over Our Oceans." *Geoengineering Watch.* 18 July. https://www.geoengineeringwatch.org/?s=climate+engineering+cover+up

Young, Ayana. 2022. "Transcript: VEDA AUSTIN on Water as Source /317." *for the wild.* 28 December. https://forthewild.world/podcast-transcripts/veda-austin-on-water-as-source-317

RESOURCES

Alfa-Vedic. "A New Living Science." (website and podcast). https://alfavedic.com/about-alfa-vedic/

Apigian, Aimie. "Do You Have a Biology of Trauma?" *Trauma Healing Accelerated* (home page). https://traumahealingaccelerated.com/

Austin, Veda. *The Secret Intelligence of Water: Science, Art & Consciousness.* (website). https://www.vedaaustin.com/

Braden, Gregg. *Awakening the Power of the New Human Story* (website). https://greggbraden.com/

Bush, John. "Live Free: Email Newsletter for people seeking freedom and prosperity." *Live Free Academy* (website). https://livefree.academy/

Bush, Zach. "Curiosity is the most powerful force on Earth." *Zach Bush MD* (website). https://zachbushmd.com/

Caffrey, Justin. "How to Change Your State." (video). https://youtube.com/shorts/9iJz5YmavXY?si=aguCBtZlzXXbDiix

Children's Health Defence. (website) https://childrenshealthdefense.org/

Childress, David Hatcher. 2024. *Ancient Advanced Technology. Gaia* (web series). https://www.gaia.com/series/ancient-advanced-technology

Christoff, Jason. "Overcoming Self-Sabotage." *J Christoff* (website). https://www.jchristoff.com/

Dispenza, Joe. "Unlimited." *Dr. Joe Dispenza* (website). https://drjoedispenza.com/

Ensworth, Heather. "A Center for Healing. . . Coming into Wholeness and Reconnecting with the Sacred in All of Life." *Rising Moon Healing Center.* https://risingmoonhealingcenter.com/

Ferrari, Alex. *Next Level Soul* (website). https://nextlevelsoul.com/about/

GetUp. 2025. *The Adani Files: New Dirt.* https://adanifiles.com.au/new-dirt

Gregory, Pam. "Astrology is Already Reflecting our Evolution of Consciousness." *The Next Step* (website). https://www.thenextstep.uk.com/

Headfulness. "Nervous System Reset." *Headfulness* (meditation video) https://youtube.com/shorts/0rFGz_5_shM?si=uNLBFJt6OMhJA2IT

Heal For Life Foundation. "Understanding Childhood Trauma." *Heal for Life* (website). https://healforlife.com.au/understanding-trauma/

Health Freedom Summit. (website) https://healthfreedomsummit.com/

HeartMath Institute. "Awaken the Heart of Humanity." *HeartMath Institute.* https://www.heartmath.org/

HeartMath Institute. "Science of the Heart: Exploring the Role of the Heart in Human Performance: An Overview of Research Conducted by the HeartMath Institute." *HeartMath Institute.* https://www.heartmath.org/research/science-of-the-heart/energetic-communication/

Homeland Security and Governmental Affairs. "Dr. Paul Makes Case for Lab Leak at First Full Senate Committee Hearing on COVID-19 Origins." *Homeland Security and Governmental Affairs.* https://www.hsgac.senate.gov/media/reps/dr-paul-makes-case-for-lab-leak-at-first-full-senate-committee-hearing-on-covid-19-origins/

Kennedy, Robert F., Jr. 2021.*The Real Anthony Fauci: Bill Gates, Big Pharma, and the Global War on Democracy and Public Health.* Skyhorse Publishing.

Ling, Alex. *Aquan: The Secret Language of Water.* https://aquan.co.uk/

Lipton, Bruce. "Bridging Science and Spirit." *Bruce H. Lipton, PhD* (website). https://www.brucelipton.com/

Mate, Gabor. "When Science Meets Compassion." *Dr. Gabor Mate* (website). https://drgabormate.com/

Mellula Yoga. "Super Fast Vagus Nerve Reset." (meditation video) https://youtube.com/shorts/kiuDg4U741Q?si=nGsZ9pPU17SGtxNq

Natawidjaja, Danny. "The Unjust Retraction of Groundbreaking Research: A Call for Academic Integrity." *Graham Hancock.* 21 March 2024. https://grahamhancock.com/natawidjajadh1/

Ortiz, Emilio. *Consciousness, Mysticism, Relationships, Health.* (YouTube channel) https://www.youtube.com/c/EmilioOrtiz

Otto, Jonathon. *Health Secret* (website). https://healthsecret.com/about/

Reidenbach, Anna. 2025. "YES Magic". https://coachannareidenbach.com/magic

Roguski, James. "Exposing MDM (Mis-Information, Dis-Information and Mal-Information)." *Substack* (blog). https://substack.com/@jamesroguski

Sandhu, Amrit. "Inspired Evolution: Do What You Love." *Amrit Sandhu* (podcast). https://inspiredevolution.com/podcast/

Shiva, Vandana. 2016. *Who Really Feeds the World? The Failures of Agribusiness and the Promise of Agroecology.* North Atlantic Books.

Tolman, Don. "The Original Don Tolman Blog." *The Original Don Tolman* (blog). https://theoriginaldontolman.com.au/blogs/the-original-don-tolman-blog

Tolman, Tyler. "7 Principles to Completely Transform Your Health." *Tyler Tolman* (blog). https://www.tylertolman.com/transform-your-health/

We Al-li, Ltd. "Culturally Informed Trauma Integrated Healing Approach." *We Al-li* (website). https://www.wealli.com.au/

Wigington, Dane. 2018. "Geoengineering: Answers To The Most Commonly Asked Questions." *GeoEngineering Watch*. 25 May. https://geoengineeringwatch.org/geoengineering-answers-to-the-most-commonly-asked-questions/

Wolf, Naomi. 2023. *Facing the Beast: Courage, Faith, and Resistance in a New Dark Age*. Chelsea Green Publishing.

Wolf, Naomi, ed. 2024. *The Pfizer Papers: Pfizer's Crimes Against Humanity*. War Room Books.

Zeck, Alec. "The Way Forward." *Substack* (blog). http://substack.com/@aleczeck

ABOUT THE AUTHOR

Elizabeth Grace first worked as a secretary/jillaroo in outback Australia. Then, she worked for an airline company in Alice Springs and eventually served as secretary to the Director of Department of Environment and Planning in Adelaide in the mid-70s, early 80s. She entered Adelaide University and completed a Bachelor of Arts in 1984, majoring in Geography. Then, she worked in the office for Coastal Protection Board and Native Vegetation Retention in the Department of Environment and Planning.

In 1986, Elizabeth trained as an Educational Kinesiologist with the EK Learning Centre. She graduated with a Master of Spiritual Science (MSS) from the Peace Theological Seminary in Los Angeles in 2000 and repeated the course work twice more from 2007 to 2010.

In 2000, she trained as a Bioresonance Therapist with Dr. Andy and Anna Barrie, *Biomed Australia,* and accredited trainers with the BICOM manufacturer Regumed in Germany. From 2019 to 2021, she trained in Transformational Coaching, Facilitation, and Leadership with Dr. Claire Zammit, Founder of the Institute for Women-Centred Coaching and Creator of Feminine Power trainings.

Elizabeth mentors women to undo the old stories from life experiences that may have kept them trapped in fear, so that they may discover their gifts and talents and blossom into their True Self, living their most authentic life.

She was previously published as a contributing author in the best-selling anthology, *Turning Point Moments*.

Elizabeth is a proud mother of two and grandmother of two beautiful girls. She is also stepmother of four, step-grandmother of nine, and enjoys a growing number of step-great grandchildren. She loves to spend time with her beloved family and circle of friends.